The Quotable Virgo

The Quotable Virgo

Virgo Traits Described by Fellow Virgos

Usual Birthdates
August 23 through September 21

Mary Valby

Quotable Zodiac Publishing, LLC
Gig Harbor, Washington

The Quotable Virgo
Virgo Traits Described by Fellow Virgos

Quotable Zodiac Publishing, LLC
Post Office Box 2011
Gig Harbor, WA 98335 USA

Orders@QuotableZodiac.com, www.QuotableZodiac.com

ISBN 978-1-936998-06-7

Design & layout: BookDesign.ca
Printed in U.S.A.
Distributed by SCB Distributors

With appreciation for my favorite Virgos
Libby and Jim

Take your needle, my child, and work at your pattern; it will come out a rose by and by. Life is like that; one stitch at a time taken patiently, and the pattern will come out all right, like embroidery.

Oliver Wendell Holmes, born 8/29/1809

The first thing I do in the morning is brush my teeth and sharpen my tongue.

Dorothy Parker, born 8/22/1893

Contents

Author's Notes about Birth Data

Data accuracy. Many famous people have different birth years published in different places. The author has checked multiple sources for accuracy and asks that data corrections be submitted to info@quotablezodiac.com.

Old Style / New Style dating. All countries in the Western world shifted from the Julian (Old Style or O.S.) to the Gregorian (New Style or N.S.) calendar, jumping ahead up to 12 days to catch up with the actual movements of the Sun. The timing of the change varied significantly by country, with France adjusting in 1582, England in 1752, and Russia in 1918. All birthdates in *The Quotable Virgo* use New Style dating to accurately reflect the astrological position of the Sun.

"On the cusp." The usual dates for a Virgo Sun are August 23 through September 21. But the Sun moves from Leo to Virgo and from Virgo to Libra at a specific moment each year, with the dates varying by a day or two from year to year. In the effort to include only true Virgos in this book, the author evaluated place of birth and time of birth where available. If you were born on the cusp and are unsure about your own Sun sign, email your date, time and place of birth to help@quotablezodiac.com for a free assessment.

Introduction

You know you're a Virgo. You identify with the standard adjectives used to describe Virgo—smart, organized, resourceful, critical. But you'd like more dimension to what being a Virgo means.

The Quotable Virgo lets your fellow Virgos tell your story. Famous Virgos describe your natural Talents for helpfulness and hard work in one chapter, addressing Challenges like isolation and anxiety in another. The section on Double-Edged Traits highlights Virgo characteristics like health concerns and giving advice that become strengths or weaknesses depending on expression. Chapters about Work, Creativity, Sports, and Relationships let you focus on Virgo tendencies within a specific arena. The core Virgo traits of intellect, practicality, discipline and longevity come through in all areas. *The Quotable Virgo* lets you select Virgo leaders, artists and athletes to identify with as you develop your own Virgo potential.

The astrological placement of Sun in Virgo at your moment of birth indicates your core energy, the life force driving the rest of your personality. From classic literature to contemporary celebrities, statements from other Virgos underscore your natural tendencies. It goes beyond coincidence that talents for hard work and consistency give Virgo the zodiac's most impressive list of long-tenured rulers. Personal reticence provides Virgo with a relatively high incidence of

reclusive celebrities. Virgo's odd humor and attention to detail make Virgo the #1 sign for famous cartoonists.

Astrology is most useful as a tool for self-knowledge, validating specific tendencies that you already perceive in yourself. Astrology describes the hand of cards that you were born with, but you put the cards into play. *The Quotable Virgo* helps you better understand yourself so that you more effectively manage your Virgo tendencies to achieve your goals.

Virgo Birthday Calendar

August 22	
1893	Dorothy Parker

August 23		August 24	
1868	Edgar Lee Masters	1591	Robert Herrick
1949	Shelley Long	1872	Max Beerbohm
1958	James Van Praagh	1884	Earl Biggers
1970	River Phoenix	1890	Jean Rhys
1976	Scott Caan	1899	Jorge Luis Borges
1978	Kobe Bryant	1903	Graham Sutherland
1988	Jeremy Lin	1910	Theodore Parker
		1924	Louis Teicher
		1929	Yasser Arafat
		1947	Paulo Coelho
		1955	Mike Huckabee
		1957	Stephen Fry
		1960	Cal Ripken Jr.
		1965	Marlee Matlin
		1973	Dave Chappelle
		1977	Alex O'Loughlin
		1978	Karrine Steffans
		1981	Chad Murray
		1988	Rupert Grint

August 25		August 26	
1530	Ivan the Terrible	1743	Antoine Lavoisier
1819	Allan Pinkerton	1819	Prince Albert (England)
1836	Bret Harte	1880	Guillaume Apollinaire
1889	William Feather	1904	Christopher Isherwood
1912	Ted Key	1906	Albert Sabin
1913	Walt Kelly	1910	Mother Teresa
1918	Leonard Bernstein	1920	Brant Parker
1919	George Wallace	1935	Geraldine Ferraro
1927	Althea Gibson	1960	Branford Marsalis
1930	Sean Connery	1970	Melissa McCarthy
1931	Regis Philbin	1980	Macaulay Culkin
1949	Gene Simmons	1980	Chris Pine
1954	Elvis Costello		
1958	Tim Burton		
1961	Billy Ray Cyrus		
1968	Rachael Ray		
1970	Jo Dee Messina		
1970	Claudia Schiffer		
1981	Rachel Bilson		
1987	Blake Lively		

August 27		August 28	
1770	Georg Hegel	1749	Goethe
1871	Theodore Dreiser	1774	St. Elizabeth Seton
1877	Lloyd Douglas	1831	Lucy Hayes
1877	Charles Rolls	1833	Edward Burne-Jones
1882	Samuel Goldwyn	1910	Morris Graves
1899	C.S. Forester	1917	Jack Kirby
1908	Lyndon Johnson	1943	Lou Piniella
1926	Oliver Lynn	1958	Scott Hamilton
1932	Antonia Fraser	1965	Shania Twain
1933	Nancy Friday	1969	Jack Black

1937	Alice Coltrane	1969	Jason Priestley
1942	Daryl Dragon	1982	LeAnn Rimes
1947	Barbara Bach	1986	Florence Welch
1952	Paul Reubens	2003	Quvenzhané Wallis
1969	Cesar Millan	2005	Honey Boo Boo
1969	Chandra Wilson		
1979	Aaron Paul		
1985	Sean Foreman		

August 29		**August 30**	
1619	Colbert	1748	Jacques-Louis David
1632	John Locke	1797	Mary Shelley
1780	Jean Ingres	1892	George Aiken
1809	Oliver Wendell Holmes	1893	Huey Long
1876	Charles Kettering	1898	Shirley Booth
1915	Ingrid Bergman	1918	Ted Williams
1920	Charlie Parker	1930	Warren Buffett
1923	Richard Attenborough	1943	Robert Crumb
1924	Dinah Washington	1946	Peggy Lipton
1936	John McCain	1951	Timothy Bottoms
1938	Elliott Gould	1963	Michael Chiklis
1939	William Friedkin	1972	Cameron Diaz
1941	Robin Leach		
1958	Michael Jackson		
1984	Paul McDonald		
1986	Lea Michele		
1993	Liam Payne		

August 31		**September 1**	
12	Caligula	1789	Marguerite Blessington
1870	Maria Montessori	1791	Lydia Howard Sigourney
1897	Fredric March	1835	William Jevons
1908	William Saroyan	1868	Kin Hubbard
1918	Alan Jay Lerner	1897	Jimmy Hatlo

1928	James Coburn	1907	Walter Reuther
1936	Marva Collins	1920	Liz Carpenter
1945	Van Morrison	1933	Ann Richards
1945	Itzhak Perlman	1933	Conway Twitty
1949	Richard Gere	1937	Lily Tomlin
1970	Queen Rania (Jordan)	1947	Barry Gibb
1971	Chris Tucker	1950	Phil McGraw
		1957	Gloria Estefan
		1970	Padma Lakshmi
		1971	Rachel Zoe
		1975	Scott Speedman

September 2		**September 3**	
1850	Eugene Field	1499	Diane de Poitiers
1850	Albert Spalding	1849	Sarah Orne Jewett
1936	Andy Grove	1860	Edward Filene
1937	Peter Ueberroth	1914	Dixy Lee Ray
1948	Christa McAuliffe	1923	Mort Walker
1951	Mark Harmon	1926	Alison Lurie
1952	Jimmy Connors	1965	Charlie Sheen
1964	Keanu Reeves	1984	Garrett Hedlund
1966	Salma Hayek		
1968	Camille Grammer		
1969	K-Ci		

September 4		**September 5**	
1634	Robert South	1638	Louis XIV (France)
1724	George Stubbs	1774	Caspar Friedrich
1803	Sarah Polk	1791	Giacomo Meyerbeer
1824	Anton Bruckner	1847	Jesse James
1905	Mary Renault	1897	Arthur Nielsen
1908	Richard Wright	1902	Darryl Zanuck
1918	Paul Harvey	1912	John Cage
1946	Liz Greene	1920	Alex Anderson

1949	Tom Watson	1927	Paul Volcker
1960	Damon Wayans	1929	Bob Newhart
1964	Anthony Weiner	1935	Joan Kennedy
1981	Beyoncé	1940	Raquel Welch
		1946	Freddie Mercury
		1950	Cathy Guisewite
		1973	Rose McGowan

September 6		**September 7**	
1634	Thomas Tryon	1782	Susan Ferrier
1757	Marquis de Lafayette	1860	Grandma Moses
1860	Jane Addams	1885	Elinor Wylie
1866	Ralph Waldo Trine	1887	George Putnam
1888	Joseph Kennedy	1887	Edith Sitwell
1944	Swoosie Kurtz	1894	Gala Dali
1947	Jane Curtin	1900	Taylor Caldwell
1954	Carly Fiorina	1905	Ivy Baker Priest
1958	Jeff Foxworthy	1909	Elia Kazan
1962	Chris Christie	1912	David Packard
1963	Alice Sebold	1921	Arthur Ferrante
1964	Rosie Perez	1936	Buddy Holly
1972	Idris Elba	1951	Chrissie Hynde
1983	Pippa Middleton	1954	Michael Emerson
		1963	Eazy-E
		1976	Oliver Hudson
		1987	Evan Rachel Wood

September 8		**September 9**	
1767	August Schlegel	1585	Cardinal Richelieu
1841	Antonin Dvorak	1828	Leo Tolstoy
1887	Swami Sivananda	1868	Mary Austin
1897	Jimmie Rodgers	1890	Colonel Sanders
1922	Sid Caesar	1900	James Hilton
1925	Peter Sellers	1911	Paul Goodman

1932	Patsy Cline	1924	Henrik Tikkanen
1971	David Arquette	1925	Cliff Robertson
1971	Brooke Burke	1951	Michael Keaton
1979	Pink	1952	Dave Stewart
1981	Jonathan Taylor Thomas	1960	Mario Batali
1987	Wiz Khalifa	1960	Hugh Grant
		1962	Kristy McNichol
		1966	Adam Sandler
		1969	Rachel Hunter
		1970	Macy Gray
		1971	Eric Stonestreet
		1972	Goran Visnjic
		1975	Michael Bublé
		1980	Michelle Williams
		1991	Hunter Hayes

September 10		**September 11**	
1839	Isaac Funk	1762	Joanna Baillie
1839	Charles Sanders Peirce	1862	O. Henry
1880	Georgia Douglas Johnson	1885	D.H. Lawrence
1890	Elsa Schiaparelli	1917	Ferdinand Marcos
1897	Georges Bataille	1924	Carol Matthau
1914	Robert Wise	1942	Lola Falana
1915	Edmond O'Brien	1950	Amy Madigan
1928	Jean Vanier	1961	Virginia Madsen
1929	Arnold Palmer	1965	Moby
1933	Karl Lagerfeld	1967	Harry Connick Jr.
1934	Charles Kuralt	1970	Taraji Henson
1960	Colin Firth	1977	Ludacris
1968	Big Daddy Kane	1981	Charles Kelley
1968	Guy Ritchie		
1974	Ryan Phillippe		

September 12		September 13	
1575	Henry Hudson	1819	Clara Schumann
1880	H.L. Mencken	1830	Marie von Ebner-Eschenbach
1888	Maurice Chevalier	1851	Walter Reed
1892	Alfred Knopf	1857	Milton Hershey
1913	Jesse Owens	1874	Arnold Schoenberg
1917	Han Suyin	1876	Sherwood Anderson
1931	George Jones	1894	J.B. Priestley
1942	Maria Muldaur	1903	Claudette Colbert
1944	Barry White	1916	Roald Dahl
1951	Joe Pantoliano	1924	Maurice Jarre
1958	Franco Amurri	1931	Barbara Bain
1959	Scott Brown	1938	Judith Martin
1962	Amy Yasbeck	1941	David Clayton-Thomas
1967	Louie C.K.	1944	Jacqueline Bisset
1971	Jessica Seinfeld	1951	Jean Smart
1974	Jennifer Nettles	1953	Iyanla Vanzant
1976	Bizzy Bone	1958	Domenico Dolce
1978	Elisabetta Canalis	1969	Tyler Perry
1981	Jennifer Hudson	1971	Stella McCartney
1986	Emmy Rossum	1977	Fiona Apple
		1993	Niall Horan

September 14		September 15	
1867	Charles Gibson	1157	Richard the Lionheart
1883	Margaret Sanger	1613	François de La Rochefoucauld
1883	Florida Scott-Maxwell	1789	James Fenimore Cooper
1891	John Striebel	1830	Porfirio Diaz
1914	Clayton Moore	1857	William Taft
1917	Sydney Harris	1890	Agatha Christie
1934	Kate Millett	1894	Jean Renoir
1944	Colleen Barrett	1903	Roy Acuff
1947	Sam Neill	1946	Tommy Lee Jones

1953	Karen Mills	1946	Oliver Stone
1960	Melissa Leo	1960	Robyn Gibson
1964	Faith Ford	1971	Josh Charles
1971	Kimberly Williams-Paisley	1979	Eric Johnson
1973	Nas	1984	Prince Harry (England)
1983	Amy Winehouse	1986	Heidi Montag

September 16		**September 17**	
1875	J.C. Penney	1533	Elizabeth I (England)
1880	Alfred Noyes	1855	David Buick
1887	Nadia Boulanger	1883	William Carlos Williams
1914	Allen Funt	1900	John Marriott
1919	Marvin Middlemark	1916	Mary Stewart
1919	Laurence Peter	1923	Hank Williams
1924	Lauren Bacall	1931	Anne Bancroft
1925	B.B. King	1935	Ken Kesey
1926	Robert Schuller	1947	Jeff MacNelly
1927	Peter Falk	1948	John Ritter
1934	George Chakiris	1953	Rita Rudner
1949	Ed Begley Jr.	1960	Kevin Clash
1952	Mickey Rourke	1965	Kyle Chandler
1956	David Copperfield	1971	Nate Berkus
1962	Baz Luhrmann		
1963	Richard Marx		
1968	Marc Anthony		
1971	Amy Poehler		
1992	Nick Jonas		

September 18		**September 19**	
1709	Samuel Johnson	1839	George Cadbury
1905	Agnes de Mille	1894	Rachel Field
1905	Greta Garbo	1911	William Golding
1940	Frankie Avalon	1933	David McCallum
1947	Drew Gilpin Faust	1934	Brian Epstein

1950	Anna Deavere Smith	1940	Paul Williams
1954	Steven Pinker	1941	Cass Elliot
1956	Debbi Fields	1948	Jeremy Irons
1961	James Gandolfini	1948	Twiggy
1964	Holly Robinson Peete	1964	Trisha Yearwood
1971	Lance Armstrong	1971	Sanaa Lathan
1971	Jada Pinkett Smith	1974	Jimmy Fallon
1975	Jason Sudeikis	1984	Kevin Zegers

September 20		**September 21**	
1878	Upton Sinclair	1645	Louis Joliet
1880	Elizabeth Kenny	1788	Margaret Taylor
1884	Maxwell Perkins	1866	H.G. Wells
1901	Gus Edson	1893	Frank Willard
1902	Stevie Smith	1909	Kwame Nkrumah
1929	Anne Meara	1931	Larry Hagman
1934	Sophia Loren	1934	Leonard Cohen
1945	Candy Spelling	1945	Jerry Bruckheimer
1967	Kristen Johnston	1947	Stephen King
		1947	Marsha Norman
		1950	Bill Murray
		1957	Ethan Coen
		1960	David James Elliott
		1965	Cheryl Hines
		1967	Faith Hill
		1968	Ricki Lake
		1971	Luke Wilson
		1981	Nicole Richie
		1984	Wale
		1989	Jason Derulo

September 22		September 23	
1791	Michael Faraday	1838	Victoria Woodhull
1895	Paul Muni	1920	Mickey Rooney
1902	John Houseman	1930	Ray Charles
1922	Chen Ning Yang		
1927	Tommy Lasorda		
1931	Fay Weldon		
1954	Shari Belafonte		
1958	Andrea Bocelli		
1960	Joan Jett		
1961	Scott Baio		
1961	Bonnie Hunt		

Talents

It is one thing to be gifted and quite another thing to be worthy of one's own gift.

Composer Nadia Boulanger, born 9/16/1887

- **Intelligence**
- **Common Sense**
- **Hard Work**
- **Consistency**
- **Morality**
- **Common Touch**
- **Service**

Intelligence

Your mind works overtime. Early Mediterranean civilizations named the fast-moving inner planet after Mercury, messenger of the gods, and assigned Mercury to the zodiac signs Virgo and Gemini. Mercury rules the mind with Virgo and Gemini the most mentally active signs of the zodiac. Gemini breezily collects superficial knowledge while Virgo delves into the details. Virgo thinks precisely and asks the questions that allow thorough

analysis. The intricate, logical plots from Virgo writers Agatha Christie (9/15/1890) and Stephen King (9/21/1947) have provided intellectual entertainment for millions.

The only fence against the world is
a thorough knowledge of it.
John Locke, born 8/29/1632

Curiosity is one of the permanent and certain
characteristics of a vigorous intellect.
Samuel Johnson, born 9/18/1709

Whatever is reasonable is true, and
whatever is true is reasonable.
Georg Hegel, born 8/27/1770

Only the thinking man lives his life, the
thoughtless man's life passes him by.
Marie von Ebner-Eschenbach, born 9/13/1830

Do not block the way of inquiry.
Charles Sanders Peirce, born 9/10/1839

Tact is after all a kind of mind-reading.
Sarah Orne Jewett, born 9/3/1849
The Country of the Pointed Firs

"But I have experimental verification,"
said the Time Traveller.
H.G. Wells, born 9/21/1866
The Time Machine

Once you've failed, analyze the problem and find out why, because each failure is one more step leading up to the cathedral of success. The only time you don't want to fail is the last time you try.

Charles Kettering, born 8/29/1876

"This affair must all be unraveled from within." He [Hercule Poirot] tapped his forehead. "These little gray cells. It is 'up to them'—as you say over here."

Agatha Christie, born 9/15/1890
The Mysterious Affair at Styles

The cure for boredom is curiosity.
There is no cure for curiosity.

Dorothy Parker, born 8/22/1893

Hornblower might not have answered quite so sharply and definitely if his curious mind had not taken note of one particular phenomenon . . . The two big lugsails were sheeted in at slightly different angles, inefficiently to the inexperienced eye. Analysis of the complicated—and desperately interesting—problem in mechanics suggested that the setting was correct.

C.S. Forester, born 8/27/1899
Hornblower During the Crisis

It is by losing himself in the objective, in inquiry, creation, and craft, that a man becomes something.

Paul Goodman, born 9/9/1911

Piggy could think. He could go step by step inside that fat head of his, only Piggy was no chief. But Piggy, for all his ludicrous body, had brains.

William Golding, born 9/19/1911
Lord of the Flies

If I have to say one word that would exemplify me as a person, as a conversationalist, as an individual, and my mental capabilities, it's my inquisitiveness. I want to know why. Why do you think that? I've always been that way.

Ted Williams, born 8/30/1918

Geeks are the cool people.

David Arquette, born 9/8/1971

I'm a closet comedy nerd. I've watched every episode of SNL since I was 13.

Ryan Phillippe, born 9/10/1974

I'm such a nerd. I listen to a lot of score music and weird instrumental stuff.

Scott Speedman, born 9/1/1975

Intelligence is a big thing. If you can't have a conversation, it's done.

Chris Pine, born 8/26/1980,
about what he wants in a girlfriend

Common Sense

Virgo stays grounded, not off in the clouds like enthusiastic Sagittarius or pushing the technological horizon like inventive Aquarius. Practical Virgo brings common sense to the situation at hand.

When speculation has done its worst, two and two still make four.

Samuel Johnson, born 9/18/1709

If you miss the first buttonhole, you will not succeed in buttoning up your coat.

Goethe, born 8/28/1749

Chance, the very worst guardian a man can choose for his personal comfort . . .

Marguerite Blessington, born 9/1/1789
The Two Friends

Science is a first-rate piece of furniture for a man's upper chamber, if he has common sense on the ground floor.

Oliver Wendell Holmes, born 8/29/1809
The Autocrat of the Breakfast-Table

Value depends entirely on utility.

William Jevons, born 9/1/1835

If you don't work, you can't play.

J.B. Priestley, born 9/13/1894
Out of Town

When you make a mistake, there are only three things you should ever do about it; 1) admit it; 2) learn from it; 3) don't repeat it.

Football coach Bear Bryant, born 9/11/1913

The best way of forgetting how you think you feel is to concentrate on what you know you know.

Mary Stewart, born 9/17/1916
This Rough Magic

The most important thing to do if you find yourself in a hole is to stop digging.

Warren Buffett, born 8/30/1930

Take what you can use and let the rest go by.
Ken Kesey, born 9/17/1935

I felt I'd earned the Good Housekeeping Seal when I designed an oval-shaped spaghetti pot because spaghetti is long.
Rachael Ray, born 8/25/1968

My most practical gadget is a Brookstone pocket knife. It has a flashlight, nail file, screwdriver and scissors. Every woman needs one!
Brooke Burke, born 9/8/1971

In my day-to-day life, I'm more about functionality.
Cameron Diaz, born 8/30/1972,
about her clothes

Hard Work

No silver spoon or overnight sensation for you! Virgo expects to work hard for what you get, putting your nose to the grindstone both physically and mentally. Early in her solo career, superstar Beyoncé (9/4/1981) earned a reputation as the hardest-working woman in show business.

I worked so hard during my childhood to meet this goal: By the time I was 30 years old, I could do what I want. I've reached that. I feel very fortunate to be in that position. But I've sacrificed a lot of things, and I've worked harder than probably anyone I know, at least in the music industry. So I just have to remind myself that I deserve it.

Beyoncé, born 9/4/1981

Labor, if it were not necessary for the existence, would be indispensable for the happiness of man.

Samuel Johnson, born 9/18/1709

Work is the true source of human welfare.

Leo Tolstoy, born 9/9/1828

No person who is enthusiastic about his work has anything to fear from life.

Samuel Goldwyn, born 8/27/1882

Reading story-books was considered slightly too pleasurable to be really virtuous. No story-books until after lunch. In the mornings you were supposed to find something "useful" to do. Even to this day, if I sit down and read a novel after breakfast I have a feeling of guilt. The same applies to cards on a Sunday.

Agatha Christie, born 9/15/1890

I'm an incredible sausage machine.

Agatha Christie, born 9/15/1890,
about producing a book a year between the World Wars

The choreographic process is exhausting. It happens on one's feet after hours of work, and the energy required is roughly the equivalent of writing a novel and winning a tennis match simultaneously.

Agnes de Mille, born 9/18/1905

Surely it's better to sleep late in the morning only when it's a rare privilege, not an everyday occurrence.

Lauren Bacall, born 9/16/1924

It seems like I always had to work harder than other people. Those nights when everybody else is asleep, and you sit in your room trying to play scales.

B.B. King, born 9/16/1925

Keep doing your job, however badly you feel about it. You can put a brand new Chrysler Town and Country in (the driveway) and say "I could buy a Ferrari, but I've chosen to do this because I'm a sensible lotto winner." Still be diligent. Still be dedicated and still work hard.

Robin Leach, born 8/29/1941

Talent is cheaper than table salt. What separates the talented individual from the successful one is a lot of hard work.

Stephen King, born 9/21/1947

I don't feel free to do what I want. It's not in my nature. I could never just do anything for fun. I feel like I've got to be productive.

Shania Twain, born 8/28/1965

I've always been a complete junkie for work.

Rachael Ray, born 8/25/1968

Consistency

Stick to your guns.

Phrase coined by Earl Biggers, born 8/24/1884

The ancients paired each zodiac sign with one of the four elements—Fire, Water, Air and Earth. Capricorn, Taurus and Virgo are Earth signs characterized by caution, practicality and stability. Capricorn persists due to ambition and Taurus endures with sheer stubbornness. Self-disciplined Virgo perseveres through the zodiac's most consistent daily routine.

Semper eadem [Ever the same].
Motto of Queen Elizabeth I, born 9/17/1533

Great works are performed, not by strength, but by perseverance. Yonder palace was raised by single stones, yet you see its height and spaciousness. He that shall walk with vigor three hours a day will pass in seven years a space equal to the circumference of the globe.

Samuel Johnson, born 9/18/1709

There are but two roads that lead to an important goal and to the doing of great things: strength and perseverance. Strength is the lot of but a few privileged men; but austere perseverance, harsh and continuous, may be employed by the least of us and rarely fails of its purpose, for its silent power grows irresistibly greater with time.

Goethe, born 8/28/1749

Come night, strike hour.
Days go, I endure.

Guillaume Apollinaire, born 8/26/1880
Le Pont Mirabeau

The race is not to the swift,
but to those that can stand still
and let the waves go over them.

D.H. Lawrence, born 9/11/1885

The big things that come our way are . . . the fruit
of seeds planted in the daily routine of our work.

William Feather, born 8/25/1889

What saved me was my stubbornness, pure stubbornness. I get stuck in ruts. I make up my mind to do something and I do it—whether it gives me pleasure or not.

Agnes de Mille, born 9/18/1905

Do not think that love, in order to be genuine, has to be extraordinary. What we need is to love without getting tired.

Mother Teresa, born 8/26/1910

If something is boring after two minutes, try it for four. If it is still boring try it for eight, sixteen, thirty-two, and so on. Eventually one discovers that it's not boring at all but very interesting.

John Cage, born 9/5/1912

Racking up nearly 17,000 hours of airtime . . . Sooner or later people get tired of you, but I've been here for nearly 29 years. I'm very proud of it.

Regis Philbin, born 8/25/1931,
about his greatest accomplishment

Of the thousands of pieces of advice, inspiration and encouragement I've received over the years, the most powerful one—the one that has played a central role in my life, both as a child and an adult—boils down to a single word: practice.

Itzhak Perlman, born 8/31/1945

Life's a marathon, not a sprint.

Phil McGraw, born 9/1/1950

I really have a strong sense—a necessity almost—for stability.

Faith Hill, born 9/21/1967

If you want to reach your goals, you need to have a plan of action. You have to stay focused on the things you can control and don't get discouraged or distracted by the things you cannot control.

Bernie Williams, born 9/13/1968

We know that discipline will turn
a princess into a queen.

Jada Pinkett Smith, born 9/18/1971
Girls Hold Up This World

Virgo Specialty: Extended Rule

Persistent effort and vigilance help Virgo leaders retain power for long periods of time. Virgo contributes more long-tenured leaders than any other astrological sign.

Virgo Leader	Birthdate	Position	Tenure
Yasser Arafat	8/24/1929	PLO chair	35 years
George Wallace	8/25/1919	Alabama Governor	16 years (4 terms)
Ferdinand Marcos	9/11/1917	Philippine President	21 years
Porfirio Diaz	9/15/1830	Mexican President	35 years
Louis XIV (France)	9/5/1638	King of France	72 years
Elizabeth I (England)	9/17/1533	Queen of England	44 years
Ivan the Terrible	8/25/1530	Russian Tsar	37 years

Morality

The constellation of the maiden was identified by the Greeks with the goddess Astraea . . . With the gradual corruption of men, Astraea conceived a hatred for the human race because of its crimes, and left earth forever, flying up to heaven to join her father Zeus and becoming the constellation of Virgo . . . She seems to be an image of the intrinsic orderliness of nature, and her disgust at humanity is a mythic image of the traditional Virgoan disgust at disorder, chaos and wastage of time and substance.

Liz Greene, born 9/4/1946

Virgo lies between Leo and Libra on the zodiac circle, providing the transition between Leo self-absorption and Libra partnership. Before interacting with others, Virgo insists upon a code of proper

behavior. As you adhere to an inner awareness of right and wrong, you strive to articulate the appropriate moral outlook.

In upright demeanor there's ever more poise
than all disguised shows of good can do.
Queen Elizabeth I, born 9/17/1533

Integrity without knowledge is weak and useless, and
knowledge without integrity is dangerous and dreadful.
Samuel Johnson, born 9/18/1709

There is not a single outward mark of courtesy
that does not have a deep moral basis.
Goethe, born 8/28/1749

Education is the art of making men ethical.
Georg Hegel, born 8/27/1770

The hero of my tale, whom I love with all the power of
my soul, whom I have tried to portray in all his beauty,
who has been, is, and will be beautiful, is Truth.
Leo Tolstoy, born 9/9/1828

For all the liberal analysis of Spencer and our modern naturalistic philosophers, we have but an infantile perception of morals. It is more involved than we, as yet, perceive. Answer, first, why the heart thrills; explain wherefore some plaintive note goes wandering about the world, undying; make clear the rose's subtle alchemy evolving its ruddy lamp in light and rain. In the essence of these facts lie the first principles of morals.
Theodore Dreiser, born 8/27/1871
Sister Carrie

Sin is a queer thing. It isn't the breaking of divine commandments. It is the breaking of one's own integrity.

D.H. Lawrence, born 9/11/1885

If you do not know the laws of right conduct, you cannot form your character.

Swami Sivananda, born 9/8/1887

Do not open your heart to evil. Because—if you do—evil will come . . . It will enter in and make its home within you, and after a little while it will no longer be possible to drive it out.

Agatha Christie, born 9/15/1890
Death on the Nile

The essence of morality is a questioning about morality; and the decisive move of human life is to use ceaselessly all light to look for the origin of the opposition between good and evil.

Georges Bataille, born 9/10/1897

In all men is evil sleeping; the good man is he who will not awaken it, in himself or in other men.

Mary Renault, born 9/4/1905
The Praise Singer

I have courage in situations that demand moral conviction. If it's right, if it's proper, I don't think of the consequences. I don't hesitate. I say: "this is goddamn unfair!" That means I am alone. But I don't mind being alone.

Agnes de Mille, born 9/18/1905

Any power is hard to hold, and power misused recoils upon the user.

Mary Stewart, born 9/17/1916
The Last Enchantment

Somebody once said that in looking for people to hire, you look for three qualities: integrity, intelligence, and energy. And if they don't have the first, the other two will kill you. You think about it; it's true. If you hire somebody without the first, you really want them to be dumb and lazy.

Warren Buffett, born 8/30/1930

If you lived your life by the Rules of Golf, you'll be a stand-up citizen. The Rules of Golf go right to your integrity as a person.

Raymond Floyd, born 9/4/1942

A mode of conduct, a standard of courage, discipline, fortitude, and integrity can do a great deal to make a woman beautiful.

Jacqueline Bisset, born 9/13/1944

I wanted to say something about moral choices, what it costs to do the right thing. The cost is high, but the cost of doing the wrong thing is higher. The suspense and horror are secondary.

Stephen King, born 9/21/1947

You have set standards for how you want to be treated and what you expect from yourself and for yourself.

Iyanla Vanzant, born 9/15/1953

It's always the question: How do you keep your integrity and stay successful?

Sanaa Lathan, born 9/19/1971

Common Touch

From the middle classes one gets ideas,
and from the common people—life itself,
warmth. You feel their hates and loves.
D.H. Lawrence, born 9/11/1885

You consider yourself the same as everyone else. Virgo is low-key, content as a cog in the wheel, gladly blending in with the crowd. Virgo doesn't want or need the extravagant style of Leo or the status symbols of Capricorn. Multi-billionaire Warren Buffett (8/30/1930) lives comfortably in a middle-class neighborhood and drives himself around. Like many young men, England's Prince Harry saw active duty in the armed forces and frequents popular night spots. Entertainer Pink (9/8/1979) usually wears her wedding ring rock down due to embarrassment at the size of her diamond.

Privilege is the greatest enemy of right.
Marie von Ebner-Eschenbach, born 9/13/1830

I hate the actor-and-the-audience business. An author should be in among the crowd, kicking their shins or cheering on to some mischief or merriment. That rather cheap seat with the gods where one sits with fellows like Anatole France and benignly looks down on the foibles, follies and frenzies of so-called fellow-men just annoys me. After all the world is not a stage—not to me: nor a theatre: nor a showhouse of any sort . . . Whoever reads me will be in the thick of the scrimmage, and if he doesn't like it—if he wants a safe seat in the audience—let him read somebody else.

D.H. Lawrence, born 9/11/1885

I've never wanted to sit in a fancy luxury box. I'm in the same seat every game, right in the midst of the crowd. And I'm there because I want to be there.

Basketball legend Red Auerbach, born 9/20/1917

I don't want to be put on a pedestal. I just want to be reasonably successful and live a normal life with all the conveniences to make it so.

Tennis champion Althea Gibson, born 8/25/1927

I'll let you in on a little secret, something I've admitted to a handful of folks. I never cared for the nickname "The King." At times, it makes me uncomfortable and even a bit irritated to be referred to that way. There is no king of golf . . . Golf is the most democratic game on earth, a pastime of the people that grants no special privileges and pays no mind to whether a man is a hotel doorman or a corporate CEO.

Arnold Palmer, born 9/10/1929

One should not be assigned one's identity in society by the job slot one happens to fill. If we truly believe in the dignity of labor, any task can be performed with equal pride because none can demean the basic dignity of a human being.

Judith Martin, born 9/13/1938

We always play clubs. It's not something that I feel above. Those are my favorite shows because they're intimate, they're tight, their sweaty, they're hot. You're close to the people. Those are my favorites.

Joan Jett, born 9/22/1960

I will . . . go along for the ride like it's Disneyland. But I'm not looking forward to wearing a tuxedo. I'm going to fail on my elegance.

Louie C.K., born 9/12/1967

You guys are champagne; I'm beer out of the bottle. I don't belong here.

Rachael Ray, born 8/25/1968,
first meeting with Food Channel executives

I choose parts because they are not glamorous. You can concentrate on your character and not have to worry about how you look.

Claudia Schiffer, born 8/25/1970

We make sure to go to restaurants or go catch a movie somewhere, drive our own cars.

Queen Rania, born 8/31/1970,
about how she and her husband try to stay grounded

Our average morning is get up, ride the dirt bikes and feed the dogs. We like the home stuff. I'm a faithful Law & Order rerunner.

Pink, born 9/8/1979

Service

The simplest and shortest ethical precept is to be served by others as little as possible and to serve others as much as possible.

Leo Tolstoy, born 9/9/1828

Egalitarianism and ethics combine to make Virgo the zodiac sign most inclined to provide service to others. Virgo wants to help.

You want to make useful contributions to the larger group. Virgo is the zodiac sign most associated with routine helpfulness to others.

Mother Teresa (8/26/1910) epitomizes Virgo service. She expanded her religious vocation to care for society's untouchables. The tireless Mother Teresa founded the Missionaries of Charity, now numbering more than 4.000 sisters who dedicate themselves to serving the poorest of the poor.

I was to leave the convent and help the poor while living among them. It was an order. To fail would have been to break the faith.

Mother Teresa, born 8/26/1910

I am a little pencil in the hand of a writing God who is sending a love letter to the world.

Mother Teresa, born 8/26/1910

Let him that desires to see others happy, make haste to give while his gift can be enjoyed, and remember that every moment of delay takes away something from the value of his benefaction.

Samuel Johnson, born 9/18/1709

A useless life is an early death.

Goethe, born 8/28/1749

Joy can be real only if people look upon their life as a service, and have a definite object in life outside themselves and their personal happiness.

Leo Tolstoy, born 9/9/1828

We teachers can only help the work going on, as servants wait upon a master.

Maria Montessori, born 8/31/1870

Great opportunities to help others seldom come, but small ones come daily.

Ivy Baker Priest, born 9/7/1905

It was just like his provision of dry clothing for me . . . It was in him, so to say, a pedestrian care which contrived much out of small things. It was a kind of science or study of domestic donation, trifles set aside, saved, little schemes, maneuvers, which he would not for the world have known to others but which must at last come to be understood by the caring recipient.

William Golding, born 9/19/1911
Fire Down Below

I'm not Miss Totally-in-control, sure of myself all the time. Why wouldn't I have the same frailties a lot of women have? I get a lot of mail from women—even young women—who consider me some sort of role model. I never set out to be one, but anytime I can do something constructive, I'm thrilled.

Lauren Bacall, born 9/16/1924

Nothing's better for getting rid of disappointment than helping someone who loves the same thing you do.

Golfer Jeff Sluman, born 9/11/1957,
helping a young golfer after losing in a playoff

I really believe that you are supposed to help out when needed and give back to your community, no matter what your financial status is.

Trisha Yearwood, born 9/19/1964

Instead of wallowing in your sorrow, if you focus on people who need you, you may do yourself the biggest favor.

Shania Twain, born 8/28/1965

I have this terrible need to tell people that they are not alone and there's something you can do. It was one of the driving forces for me to write this book, and I think maybe it's keeping me sober.

Kristen Johnston, born 9/20/1967

I'm not going to be some person in the royal family who just finds a lame excuse to go abroad and do all sorts of sunny holidays and whatever. I can see myself doing as much as I can in the position that I've got.

Prince Harry, born 9/15/1984

Virgo Specialty: Practical Assistance

Virgo contributes useful services to those in need.

- Twice weekly, David Arquette (9/8/1971) serves food at a local mission
- Salma Hayek (9/2/1966) and Jada Pinkett Smith (9/18/1971) actively campaign against domestic violence to women
- Jean Vanier (9/10/1928) founded l'Arche, a federation of group homes for the developmentally disabled
- George Aiken (8/30/1892) fathered food stamps
- Margaret Sanger (9/14/1883) crusaded for women's contraception as an essential health service.
- By treating polio with muscle exercise, Elizabeth Kenny (8/20/1880) laid the foundation for contemporary physical therapy
- Upton Sinclair (9/20/1878) wrote *The Jungle* to expose the meat industry's harsh working conditions
- Hull House founder Jane Addams (9/6/1860) baked bread for the poor and lobbied for fair labor laws
- St. Elizabeth Seton (8/28/1774) established religious communities to care for poor children
- The Vestal Virgins guarded the sacred flame of ancient Rome

Nothing could be worse than the fear that one had given up too soon, and left one unexpended effort that might have saved the world.

Jane Addams, born 9/6/1860

No woman can call herself free until she can choose consciously whether she will or will not be a mother.

Margaret Sanger, born 9/14/1883

Double-Edged Traits

- Detail
- Advice
- Adaptability
- Sexuality
- Health Perceptions

Detail

Virgo is the zodiac's micromanager, more attentive to detail than any other sign. Your talents for analysis and hard work ensure that every little thing is examined and adjusted as needed. Detective Hercule Poirot from Agatha Christie (9/15/1890) solves crimes by cleverly connecting the dots between seemingly unrelated details. But the immaculately-tailored Poirot is fussy regarding food and snobbish about manners. Virgo exactitude can disenfranchise others, and your perfectionism can hold you back from taking action.

The true art of memory is the art of attention.
Samuel Johnson, born 9/18/1709

Life is a great bundle of little things.
Oliver Wendell Holmes, born 8/29/1809

True life is lived when tiny changes occur.
Leo Tolstoy, born 9/9/1828

To succeed in life every detail should be arranged well beforehand.
Agatha Christie, born 9/15/1890
Death on the Nile

Watch every detail that affects the accuracy of your work.
Researcher Arthur Nielsen, born 9/5/1897

Be faithful in small things because it is in them that your strength lies.
Mother Teresa, born 8/26/1910

I'm forever fussing with the golf course, changing this or adding that to try to make it an even more special golfing experience for those who play it.
Arnold Palmer, born 9/10/1929,
about a golf course he owns

I have our entire relationship saved on my phone. Sixteen messages between meeting and getting married. I resave them every 21 days.
Rachael Ray, born 8/25/1968

I'm all about the little things: window treatments, nice picture frames, stuff like that.
David Arquette, born 9/8/1971

I'm a Virgo and I'm really good at scheduling. And I really make it work.

Nicole Richie, born 9/21/1981

It is completely unimportant. That is why it is so interesting.

Agatha Christie, born 9/15/1890
The Murder of Roger Ackroyd

Unimportant, irrelevant, resolutely insignificant . . .

Charles Kuralt, born 9/10/1934,
describing his On the Road broadcast segments

I'm obsessed. I want it to be Christmas everywhere you look, with every little detail covered.

Faith Ford, born 9/14/1964

Those who apply themselves too closely to little things often become incapable of great things.

François de La Rochefoucauld, born 9/15/1613

Surely life, if it is long, is tedious, since we are forced to call in the assistance of so many trifles to rid us of our time.

Samuel Johnson, born 9/18/1709

Since the great thing for enabling one to get through work is regularity, he had carried regularity in his life to the highest point of exactitude. His meals were served in a fixed and invariable manner, and not only at a certain hour, but at a certain minute.

Leo Tolstoy, born 9/9/1828
War and Peace

Crude classifications and false generalizations are the curse of organized life.

H.G. Wells, born 9/21/1866

It's pretty hard to be efficient without being obnoxious.
Kin Hubbard, born 9/1/1868

If you wait for the perfect moment when all is safe and assured, it may never arrive. Mountains will not be climbed, races won, or lasting happiness achieved.
Maurice Chevalier, born 9/12/1888

He always wanted to be perfect. And when he wasn't, he'd get mad.
about Ted Williams, born 8/30/1918,
reported by a Florida fishing guide

I've long believed that if you're looking for that perfect partner you're making a big mistake. If you can find an 80 percent fit and hope that you'll grow together on the other 20 percent, you'll find happiness a lot quicker. You wait for a 100 percent partner and you're going to be looking a long time, maybe forever.
Phil McGraw, born 9/1/1950

Part of the reason I didn't tour on the last album is that I knew what it could be like if you have the right lights and the right sound and the right production. And I didn't want to do a show unless I could reach a standard I had set for myself.
Shania Twain, born 8/28/1965

Virgo Specialty: Reputation as a "Perfectionist"

- Beyoncé (9/4/1981)
- Faith Hill (9/21/1967)
- Hugh Grant (9/9/1960)
- Michael Jackson (8/29/1958)
- Richard Gere (8/31/1949)
- Lauren Bacall (9/16/1924)

The creative urge is the demon that will
not accept anything second-rate.
Agnes de Mille, born 9/18/1905

There is no defense against a perfect
pass. I can throw the perfect pass.
Dan Marino, born 9/15/1961

I'm chasing perfection.
Kobe Bryant, born 8/23/1978

Advice

It seems like one of the hardest lessons to
be learned in this life is where your business
ends and somebody else's begins.
Kin Hubbard, born 9/1/1868

Virgo sees the problem and puzzles through to a solution. Warren Buffett (8/30/1930), Phil McGraw (9/1/1950) and Rachael Ray (8/25/1968) dispense practical, digestible advice. Virgo's active, analytical mind overflows into recommendations for others. You intend to be helpful, but your nonstop suggestions can annoy and irritate others. Virgo easily turns into the busybody poking your nose into everyone else's business.

One gives nothing so freely as advice.
François de La Rochefoucauld, born 9/15/1613

Advice . . . always gives a temporary
appearance of superiority.
Samuel Johnson, born 9/18/1709

If a man hasn't got plenty of good common sense,
the more science he has the worse for his patient.
Oliver Wendell Holmes, born 8/29/1809

If you want to get rid of somebody just tell
'em something for their own good.
Kin Hubbard, born 9/1/1868

Good advice is always certain to be ignored,
but that's no reason not to give it.
Agatha Christie, born 9/15/1890

Don't waste your time with explanations:
people only hear what they want to hear.
Paulo Coelho, born 8/24/1947

I don't want to give any advice to a 19-year-old, because I want a 19-year-old to make mistakes and learn from them. Make mistakes, make mistakes, make mistakes. Just make sure they're your mistakes.
Fiona Apple, born 9/13/1977

I'm really nosy, and I'm desperate for drama, so
I'm always like "Tell me, tell me, tell me."
Nicole Richie, born 9/21/1981

Adaptability

Tradition divides zodiac signs into three types of action—Cardinal (dynamic), Fixed (purposeful) and Mutable (adaptable). Mutable signs Virgo, Pisces, Sagittarius and Gemini share the ability to adapt to the circumstances. Virgo openness allows positive change and finds immediate solutions. But sometimes you pursue each new idea too far. Analyzing each piece without knitting the pieces together lets you lose the forest for the trees. Virgo must learn to prioritize.

The same man will, indeed, often see and judge the same things differently on different occasion: early convictions must give way to more mature ones.

Goethe, born 8/28/1749

Don't be "consistent," but be simply true.

Oliver Wendell Holmes, born 8/29/1809

The desert floras shame us with their cheerful adaptations to the seasonal limitations. Their whole duty is to flower and to fruit, and they do it hardly, or with tropical luxuriance, as the rain admits . . . One hopes the land may breed like qualities in her human offspring, not tritely to "try," but to do.

Mary Austin, born 9/9/1868
The Land of Little Rain

Everything is change, and you cannot step twice into the same river.

Mary Renault, born 9/4/1905
The Last of the Wine

I really can't hate more than five or ten years. Wouldn't it be terrible to be always burdened with those primary emotions you had at one time?

Han Suyin, born 9/12/1917

Approach the game with no preset agendas and you'll probably come away surprised at your overall efforts.

Basketball coach Phil Jackson, born 9/17/1945

I have a lot of chameleon qualities. I get very absorbed in my surroundings.

River Phoenix, born 8/23/1970

There are no conditions to which a man cannot become accustomed.

Leo Tolstoy, born 9/9/1828

One may no more live in the world without picking up the moral prejudices of the world than one will be able to go to hell without perspiring.

H.L. Mencken, born 9/12/1880

True, I've been a long time making up my mind, but now I'm giving you a definite answer. I won't say yes, and I won't say no—but I'm giving you a definite maybe.

Samuel Goldwyn, born 8/27/1882

I am not and never shall be a good conversationalist; I am so easily suggestible that I have to get away by myself before I know what I really think or need to do.

Agatha Christie, born 9/15/1890

Sanity is the lot of those who are most obtuse, for lucidity destroys one's equilibrium: it is unhealthy to honestly endure the labors of the mind which incessantly contradict what they have just established.

Georges Bataille, born 9/10/1897

For God's sake, don't say yes until I've finished talking.

Darryl Zanuck, born 9/5/1902

What you are saying just proves that I have been unenterprising. I find it difficult getting things started. I think too long . . . I have always needed someone to give me a push.

Greta Garbo, born 9/18/1905

*He's as finicky as the five-times-
table, and about as lively.*

Mary Stewart, born 9/17/1916
Nine Coaches Waiting

The mind plays tricks on you. The memories change. Your attitudes change. People tell you so much about yourself, you start to half believe what they read, rather than what you lived. Happens even to a curmudgeon like me.

Ted Williams, born 8/30/1918

*If I just looked at the pluses and minuses, I'd
never leave—it's an eight-column decision.*

Jason Sudeikis, born 9/18/1975,
about returning to Saturday Night Live

Sexuality

Virgo contributes the traditional sex symbols Sophia Loren (9/20/1934), Raquel Welch (9/5/1940) and Richard Gere (8/31/1949). Sexual promise contributes to Virgo charm. A series of books by Nancy Friday (8/27/1933) opened up the sexual vistas of an entire generation. But sexuality usually leaves Virgo vaguely uncomfortable. Your attempts at sexual self-expression may include aversion to sex, androgyny, or overzealous pursuit of sex. For best results, the Virgo harvest should occur at the proper time in the proper manner.

*If a few lustful and erotic reveries make the
housework go by "as if in a dream," why not?*

Nancy Friday, born 8/27/1933

*Sex appeal is 50 percent what you've got and
50 percent what people think you've got.*

Sophia Loren, born 9/20/1934

Sexiness should not be overt. Something shapeless that drapes across your hip, hangs off the shoulder; something that cowls in the front, drapes low in the back, that's sexy.

Rachel Zoe, born 9/1/1971

I think sex is something people should study. They study everything else—why not sex? You should make an effort to know every single thing you can about it.

Brooke Burke, born 9/8/1971

I'm boy crazy. I love boys!

Cameron Diaz, born 8/30/1972,
about playing the field

I'm very conscious of being a curvy woman, and I'm very happy that I am.

Beyoncé, born 9/4/1981

Man can endure earthquake, epidemic, dreadful disease, every form of spiritual torment; but the most dreadful tragedy that can befall him is and will remain the tragedy of the bedroom.

Leo Tolstoy, born 9/9/1828

While we think of it, and talk of it
Let us leave it alone, physically, keep apart.
For while we have sex in the mind, we truly
have none in the body.

D.H. Lawrence, born 9/11/1885
Leave Sex Alone

Aren't women prudes if they don't and prostitutes if they do?

Kate Millett, born 9/14/1934

I bought sultry lingerie but I'm too embarrassed to wear it. I bought a suggestive card, but I'm too embarrassed to give it. I thought of renting a sexy movie, but I'm too embarrassed to go pick one out and even if I did, I'd be too embarrassed to admit I had it. I'm beginning to understand why red is the color of Valentine's Day.

Cathy Guisewite, born 9/5/1950

It doesn't plague me like it used to. Just the teenageriness of it, how immature it was, that people would think that I was this character. In the beginning, it was a hard load to bear being slutty and tawdry and sexy. That was really confusing for my self-image at that age.

Michelle Williams, born 9/9/1980

I should like to know why nearly every man that approaches greatness tends to homosexuality, whether he admits it or not.

D.H. Lawrence, born 9/11/1885

I am as gay as a daffodil, my dear.

Freddie Mercury, born 9/5/1946

You can say that I'm different, that I'm freaky, that I'm weird—you can say lots of stuff about me. But you can't say I'm a pedophile. That's just not a part of who I am. I am not a child pornographer.

Paul Reubens, born 8/27/1952

I'm not saying no, I'm not saying yes. I'm saying believe what you want. Assume away.

Joan Jett, born 9/22/1960,
on persistent rumors about her sexuality

I change my mind so much I need two boyfriends and a girlfriend.

Pink, born 9/8/1979

I like the androgyny of it. Same with the vests. Men's tailoring makes things cooler, and it's also sexy in an understated way.

Rachel Bilson, born 8/25/1981,
about a white shirt with a black tie

I've honestly fallen in love with a man and I've honestly fallen in love with a woman . . . I don't know how you label that, it's just how it is.

Evan Rachel Wood, born 9/7/1987

About 15 times, a lady has said, "It's either me or Lucille [his guitar]. That's why I've had 15 children by 15 women."

B.B. King, born 9/16/1925

I always had a crush on cheerleaders. Catholic cheerleaders—my double favorite.

Hugh Grant, born 9/9/1960,
on his fetish

I never did drugs and I can't really drink because I have zero tolerance for alcohol, so my vice became women. I was never faithful to most of them . . . I started doing it because I was a normal heterosexual guy and I could. Then it snowballs to where it's all about the game.

Actor-director Scott Baio, born 9/22/1961

Virgo Specialty: Confused Sexual Boundaries

Sexual intensity makes Scorpio the sign most likely to be one-dimensionally identified with sex. Sexual uncertainty makes Virgo the zodiac sign most subject to accusations of strange sex-related offenses.

- A sexual assault allegation against Kobe Bryant (8/23/1978) was eventually dismissed
- Charlie Sheen (9/3/1965) enjoys relationships with multiple porn stars
- A sexting scandal disrupted the promising political career of U.S. Congressman Anthony Weiner (9/4/1964)
- Hugh Grant (9/9/1960) and Edwin Moses (8/31/1955) were charged with soliciting prostitution
- Michael Jackson (8/29/1958) fought accusations of seducing young boys
- The children's television careers of Paul Reubens (8/27/1952) and Kevin Clash (9/17/1960) were derailed by sexual allegations
- Actress Ingrid Bergman (8/29/1915) and educator Maria Montessori (8/31/1870) suffered severely damaged reputations when they bore children out of wedlock
- D.H. Lawrence (9/11/1885) wrote novels about individuals not knowing what to do with their sexuality. Lawrence's publisher was put on trial for violating obscenity laws.
- The novels of Theodore Dreiser (8/27/1871) were publicly censored because of their sexual promiscuity

Why can't you share your bed? The most loving thing to do is to share your bed with someone. It's very charming. It's very sweet. It's what the whole world should do.

Michael Jackson, born 8/29/1958

Virgo's inner morality, when it is genuinely inner and not borrowed from the prevailing collective . . . is not at odds with what might be considered rather unconventional sexual behavior . . . Bestowing one's gifts or one's bounty as one wishes, according to inner laws, rather than satisfying expectations to gain rewards, seems fundamental to the mythic figure or the Virgin.

Liz Greene, born 9/4/1946

Health Perceptions

Virgo develops healthy habits appropriate to the zodiac's most health-conscious sign. Virgo celebrities Greta Garbo (9/18/1905), Leonard Bernstein (8/25/1918) and Anne Bancroft (9/17/1931) pursued exercise routines and healthy diets long before they were fashionable. But constant preoccupation with health makes you inclined to hypochondria. Michael Jackson (8/29/1958) and Jimmy Connors (9/2/1952) were notorious for cancelling scheduled appearances due to apparent ailments. More than other signs, Virgo frets about upcoming illness.

Walks are good for the head. They put you in a good mood and help you avoid being depressed.

Greta Garbo, born 9/18/1905

Happiness is good health—and a bad memory.

Ingrid Bergman, born 8/29/1915

Exercise makes you more graceful. When you exercise you walk as if you own the street—with pride and fluidity.

Sophia Loren, born 9/20/1934

Now that I'm over 40 I'm beginning to exercise,
I do what I can when I can . . . I still juice for
a couple of days, maybe twice a year.

Salma Hayek, born 9/2/1966

For everything to click, my weight and diet have to be right, and I can't have any negative elements in my life. Cyclists should live like monks: eat, sleep, ride. My life's not like that now, but it used to be.

Lance Armstrong, born 9/18/1971

For me, being strong is a mental buildup. My body is my temple, and you have to take care of the body in order to take care of the mind. If you're physically strong, it's also exercise for your mind.

Jada Pinkett Smith, born 9/18/1971

I will do pretty much any sport. I snowboard and ski and run and work out with my trainer as much as possible. It's really important to feel strong and fit and healthy.

Cameron Diaz, born 8/30/1972

I'm all about health.

Lea Michele, born 8/29/1986

There can be no folly greater than by fearing that which is not, nor by overgrieving for that which needs not, to overthrow at one instant the health of mind and body, which once being lost, the rest of our life is labor and sorrow, a work to God unacceptable, and to our friends discomfortable.

Queen Elizabeth I, born 9/17/1533

If a man thinks about his physical or moral state, he usually discovers that he is ill.

Goethe, born 8/28/1749

For D.H. Lawrence, existence was one continuous convalescence; it was as though he were newly re-born from a mortal illness every day of his life.

About D.H. Lawrence, born 9/11/1885
from Aldous Huxley

Thinking of disease constantly will intensify it. Feel always "I am healthily in body and mind."

Swami Sivananda, born 9/8/1887

Beastly things, teeth. Give us trouble from the cradle to the grave.

Agatha Christie, born 9/15/1890

I have to be in motion for at least an hour, preferably two, every day. I was a frail child and I have often been ill throughout my life. I think I grew too quickly.

Greta Garbo, born 9/18/1905

I caught a real bad cold driving to Sarasota—I always had respiratory problems—and was so sick I had to spend three days in New Orleans before I could drive on.

Ted Williams, born 8/30/1918

Using pain pills when you don't need them is worrisome, but you block it out.

Kristen Johnston, born 9/20/1967

How few of his friends' houses would a man choose to be at when he is sick.

Samuel Johnson, born 9/18/1709

One's own surroundings means so much to one, when one is feeling miserable.

Edith Sitwell, born 9/7/1887

Whenever I go into a house, the first thing I think is, "Would I want to be sick there? Would I want to be there on a rainy day?" [I like] cozy.

Nicole Richie, born 9/21/1981

Challenges

The man with insight enough to admit his limitations comes nearest to perfection.
Goethe, born 8/28/1749

Growth begins when we start to accept our own weakness.
Jean Vanier, born 9/10/1928

- **Reserve**
- **Fleeing the Spotlight**
- **Anxiety**
- **Extreme Behavior**
- **Complaints**
- **Criticism**
- **Crassness**

Reserve

We ought not to isolate ourselves, for we cannot remain in a state of isolation. Social intercourse makes us the more able to bear with ourselves and with others.
Goethe, born 8/28/1749

But you want to isolate. Virgo starts out shy, uncertain, anything but assertive. You find you have nothing to say, so you're not much of a party person. Virgo needs time before choosing to open up; others perceive you as remote and distant. The Latin word for Virgo translates as "self-contained."

Silence propagates itself, and the longer talk has been suspended, the more difficult it is to find anything to say.
Samuel Johnson, born 9/18/1709

I'm exhausted from not talking.
Samuel Goldwyn, born 8/27/1882

"But why didn't you ever tell me?" asked mother, I hesitated, mustering all my dignity, and proclaimed: "I don't care for parting with information". This was incomprehensible to the rest of my family, who were all extrovert talkers.
Agatha Christie, born 9/15/1890

Don't talk unless you can improve the silence.
Jorge Luis Borges, born 8/24/1899

Well, gentlemen. As usual I have nothing to say!
Greta Garbo, born 9/18/1905

A room is a place where you hide from the wolves outside and that's all any room is.
Jean Rhys, born 8/24/1890
Good Morning, Midnight

What I really need is a good old-fashioned ivory tower.
Mary Stewart, born 9/17/1916
The Stormy Petrel

When I tried to enter the private room reserved for the party, I was turned back. "No admission yet, Madam. Another twenty minutes before anyone is allowed to go in." I retreated. Why I couldn't say outright, "I am Mrs. Christie and I have been told to go in," I don't know. It was because of my miserable, horrible inevitable shyness.

Agatha Christie, born 9/15/1890

I'm more the sort that asks timidly, "If you possibly have the time and it's quite convenient, could you please . . ."

Cheryl Hines, born 9/21/1965

I'm not a naturally assertive person.

Dave Chappelle, born 8/24/1973

Everyone old enough to have a secret is entitled to have some place to keep it.

Judith Martin, born 9/13/1938

When I'm performing I'm an extrovert, yet inside I'm a completely different man.

Freddie Mercury, born 9/5/1946

Oh, yes. I am not going to talk about it with you, though.

Tommy Lee Jones, born 9/15/1946

I'd rather just do the show and go live my life privately . . . I'm not good at all in small crowds.

Tyler Perry, born 9/13/1969

You protect those things that are sacred and personal to you.

Jennifer Nettles, born 9/12/1974

We like to keep some things private. We appreciate it when people respect that. Everyone has a right to his own business.

Nick Jonas, born 9/16/1992

Company was irksome to me; when alone, I could fill my mind with the sights of heaven and earth . . . But busy uninteresting joyous faces brought back despair to my heart. I saw an unsurmountable barrier placed between me and my fellow-men.

Mary Shelley, born 8/30/1797
Frankenstein

She was hardly more affable than a cameo.

Max Beerbohm, born 8/24/1872
Zuleika Dobson

I'm not a party girl. I don't even drink.

Shania Twain, born 8/28/1965

I had an epiphany a few years ago where I was out at a celebrity party and it suddenly dawned on me that I had yet to meet a celebrity who is as smart and interesting as any of my friends.

Moby, born 9/11/1965

I'm not a nightclub guy at all. I wake up at 5 a.m. every day and go to bed early.

Scott Caan, born 8/23/1976

I'm not really a big going-out girl.

Lea Michele, born 8/29/1986

I had a lot of friends in high school, but I was never the wild party girl. Never have been, never plan to be!

Blake Lively, born 8/25/1987

It was miserable. I was much happier when I was by myself. 'Cause I mean, when you have to change yourself that much, you are not yourself anymore, so what's the point, really?

Evan Rachel Wood, born 9/7/1987

Avoid the reeking herd,
Shun the polluted flock,
Live like that stoic bird,
The eagle of the rock.
If in the eagle's track
Your sinews cannot leap,
Avoid the lathered pack,
Turn from the steaming sheep.
If you would keep your soul
From spotted sight or sound,
Live like the velvet mole;
Go burrow underground.

Elinor Wylie, born 9/7/1885
The Eagle and the Mole

Fleeing the Spotlight

You have no desire to call attention to yourself. Except for practiced performances, Virgo doesn't want the center of the stage. Virgo celebrities dislike the trappings of fame and wish for a return to anonymity.

It had everything that is most awful about parties: masses of people, television, lights, photographers, reporters, speeches, this, that and the other—nobody in the world was more inadequate to act the heroine than I was.

Agatha Christie, born 9/15/1890

I give them everything I've got on the screen—
why do they try to usurp my privacy?
Greta Garbo, born 9/18/1905

It's a strange thing, this television. God didn't design anyone to be recognized by two billion people.
Peter Falk, born 9/16/1927

My wife and I made a conscious decision not to be on the A list, and we easily could have been.
Bob Newhart, born 9/5/1929

My basic instinct is to go into my room, shut the door and have privacy. That my life has gone in the direction it has, well, I can't even believe it!
Richard Gere, born 8/31/1949

I am a hermit and would rather do other things, like work on my son's homework.
Jean Smart, born 9/13/1951,
about avoiding the Hollywood scene

At any point in an actor's life, to have made a genuine impact is something to be cherished. But I get the jitters if too much attention is focused on me.
Colin Firth, born 9/10/1960

I wanted to be that bird back in the tree looking down on the world. As opposed to, I don't know, the bird on the street getting run over by a truck.
Alice Sebold, born 9/6/1963,
after sudden fame

I don't want to be superfamous,
man. That would be awful.

Keanu Reeves, boı

I'm in a great position now where I've got
recognition. I'm not recognized too much.

Kyle Chandler, born 9/17/1965

I just didn't think the whole "famous" thing through well enough. I assumed that one could be "famous" whenever one felt like it, then go back to normal the rest of the time. It was a sad day when I had to acknowledge that I loved everything about being a FAMOUS ACTRESS except the FAMOUS part.

Kristen Johnston, born 9/20/1967

I walk out in the morning, and the UPS guy tells me
to go get 'em or something. It's fine, but . . . there's
definitely something to be said for anonymity.

Mike Piazza, born 9/4/1968

For a reserved person like me, being thrust into the
limelight took a lot of adjustment and courage.
The thought of a public life made me nervous.

Queen Rania, born 8/31/1970,
preparing to wed the future King of Jordan

People think I'm strong, but actually I wanted to crawl
away. I thought, I'm going to live in the country with
my horse and I'll get a nine-to-five; I don't need this.

Stella McCartney, born 9/13/1971

I don't want to be promoted. I'm already too much promoted. I want to be unknown. I don't want to go and [have] people recognize me everywhere. I try to do as [little] as I can. It's already enough.

Tennis player Gustavo Kuerten, born 9/10/1976

Something I have to get used to . . .

Basketball star Yao Ming, born 9/12/1980,
about life in the spotlight

I definitely have a shy component. I think all actors do. There's a part of you that wants to be seen and heard, but then you want to retreat.

Chris Pine, born 8/26/1980

Becoming too famous. I want to go on vacations and do special things. I want my privacy.

Beyoncé, born 9/4/1981,
about what really freaks her out

I have reclusive tendencies. I can hide like the best of them.

Garrett Hedlund, born 9/3/1984

Virgo Specialty: #2 in Famous Recluses

Virgo trails only guarded Capricorn in famously private celebrities.

- Actress Greta Garbo (9/18/1905) refused to grant interviews or attend her own movie premieres
- Baseball all-star Ted Williams (8/30/1918) kept the press at arm's length because he couldn't stand prying and criticism
- Actor Bill Murray (9/21/1950) has no agent or manager and can only be reached through a private phone number
- Michael Jackson (8/29/1958) kept to himself

- After becoming Hollywood's highest-paid actor, comedian Chris Tucker (8/31/1971) took a five-year hiatus from film
- Dave Chappelle (8/24/1973) abruptly quit his Comedy Central show for a trip to Africa

Coming here I don't have the distractions of fame. It quiets the ego down.

Dave Chappelle, born 8/24/1973

I have walked most of the paths in this area and I have almost always done it alone. I am a recluse.

Greta Garbo, born 9/18/1905

She retired from the world for good an' all, though she was a well-off woman. All she wanted was to get away from folks; she thought she wasn't fit to live with anybody, and wanted to be free. Shell-heap Island come to her from her father, and first thing folks knew she'd gone off out there to live, and left word she didn't want no company.

Sarah Orne Jewett, born 9/3/1849
The Country of the Pointed Firs

Anxiety

Virgo worries. The constant churning of your busy mind keeps you highstrung and anxious. Virgo celebrities fret over the obligatory talk show appearances.

Generally, I would like not to do talk shows at all because they make me very nervous, because I'm playing Swoosie and not a role.

Swoosie Kurtz, born 9/6/1944

The big talk shows: the Lenos and Lettermans. You don't have to be smart, but you have to have something. There's a lot of pressure. I start trying to think something up to say about a month in advance.

Jack Black, born 8/28/1969,
about what makes him nervous

To tremble before anticipated evils is to bemoan what thou hast never lost.

Goethe, born 8/28/1749

Some people bear three kinds of trouble—the ones they've had, the ones they have, and the ones they expect to have.

H.G. Wells, born 9/21/1866

Never any relaxing, never any leaving himself to the great hunger and impersonality of passion; he must be brought back to a deliberate, reflective creature.

D.H. Lawrence, born 9/11/1885

After ten years of experience, Hornblower knew he should have more sense than to fret himself into a fever over winds, the uncontrollable, unpredictable winds that had governed his life since boyhood. But here he was fretting himself into a fever.

C.S. Forester, born 8/27/1899
Hornblower During the Crisis

I'm not much of a golfer. I don't have any friends. And, all I like to do the day of a game is go home and be alone and worry about ways not to lose.

Bear Bryant, born 9/11/1913

You can't start worrying about what's going to happen. You get spastic enough worrying about what's happening now.

Lauren Bacall, born 9/16/1924

I really do need some relaxation, I'm just not very good at vacationing.

Jack Black, born 8/28/1969

People are always like, "Oh, you're such a laid-back guy." And I'll think, "I wish I was." Maybe it's because I talk slow.

Luke Wilson, born 9/21/1971

I am a person who has a hard time shutting off my brain.

Beyoncé, born 9/4/1981

I'm never satisfied, man. I'm Virgo. We overanalyze and we're never satisfied. So I'm gonna keep going 'til the wheels fall off.

Rapper Wale, born 9/21/1984

'Tain't worthwhile to wear a day all out before it comes.

Sarah Orne Jewett, born 9/3/1849
The Country of the Pointed Fir

You cannot play the game of life with sweaty palms.

Phil McGraw, born 9/1/1950

I'd like to just be a little bit more open to making mistakes and not worrying about it so much.

Joan Jett, born 9/22/1960

Extreme Behavior

Virgo anxiety erupts into extreme behavior. Dramatic Leo acts up with confidence and style. But Virgo antics are loud, awkward explosions as pent-up tensions reach the boiling point. Charlie Sheen (9/3/1965) was fired from his long-running TV series after trashing a hotel room and acknowledging his use of prostitutes and illegal drugs. Sheen added fuel to the flames with his tour "My Violent Torpedo of Truth / Defeat is Not An Option," intended to be humorous but cancelled due to minimal appeal. The release of Virgo tension leaves others questioning your sanity.

It is a big day of gladness at the Sober Valley Lodge
because now I can take all of their bazillions . . .
and I never have to put on those silly shirts as long
as this warlock exists in the terrestrial dimension.

Charlie Sheen, born 9/3/1965

I take things too far, that's who I am.

Charlie Sheen, born 9/3/1965

Insanity is often the logic of an
accurate mind overtasked

Oliver Wendell Holmes, born 8/29/1809
The Autocrat of the Breakfast Table

I am not eccentric. It's just that I am more
alive than most people. I am an unpopular
electric eel set in a pond of goldfish.

Edith Sitwell, born 9/7/1887

I was much too far out all my life
And not waving but drowning.

Stevie Smith, born 9/20/1902
Not Waving But Drowning

Truly great madness cannot be achieved without significant intelligence.

Finnish writer Henrik Tikkanen, born 9/9/1924

But I think that sometime, when one's behaved like a rather second-rate person, the way I did at breakfast, then in a kind of self-destructive shock one goes and does something really second-rate. Almost as if to prove it.

Novelist Alison Lurie, born 9/3/1926

I was always carrying on in the hallways. I used to twist this one kid's feet when he was asleep. I thought it was such a scream.

Regis Philbin, born 8/25/1931,
about his college days

If only no one had told them I was mad. Then I wouldn't be.

Kate Millett, born 9/14/1934
The Loony-Bin Trip

I think the big danger of madness is not madness itself, but the habit of madness. What I discovered during the time I spent in the asylum is that I could choose madness and spend my whole life without working, doing nothing, pretending to be mad. It was a very strong temptation.

Paulo Coelho, born 8/24/1947

I'm the definition of decadence.

21-year-old Charlie Sheen, born 9/3/1965

Reserved people might have a problem with loud, goofy Rachael Ray. Well, I've got a problem with people who are too quiet.

Rachael Ray, born 8/25/1968

There are only so many tables you can dance on, and as far as I'm concerned, I put my name on all of them.

Pink, born 9/8/1979

Complaints

Your mental tension spills into the three C's of Virgo's verbal challenge—complaints, criticism and crassness. Virgo is the whiner of the zodiac. The world will hear your concerns. Famous Virgos complain about the inconvenience of continued success.

It is as bad as bad can be; it is ill-fed, ill-killed, ill-kept, and ill-drest.

Samuel Johnson, born 9/18/1709,
about the mutton served at a local inn

Of all noises, I think music is the least disagreeable.

Samuel Johnson, born 9/18/1709

Petty ills, like a troop of locusts, making up by their number and their stings what they want in magnitude.

Scottish novelist Susan Ferrier, born 9/7/1782
Marriage

Life is made up of sobs, sniffles, and smiles, with sniffles predominating.

O. Henry, born 9/11/1862

Every year, back comes spring, with nasty little birds yapping their fool heads off and the ground all mucked up with plants.

Dorothy Parker, born 8/22/1893

If there is a 50-50 chance that something can go wrong, then nine times out of ten it will.

Paul Harvey, born 9/4/1918

Man invented language to satisfy
his deep need to complain.

Lily Tomlin, born 9/1/1937

They usually have two tellers in my local bank,
except when it's very busy, when they have one.

Rita Rudner, born 9/17/1953

Sometimes when I look in the mirror, I see a child,
then I look and I see a woman who should be turning
60. I've always taken care of everyone else, and I
think I've buried some issues for a long time.

LeAnn Rimes, born 8/28/1982

Every time I create an appointment, I create
a hundred malcontents and one ingrate.

Louis XIV, born 9/5/1638

Why is it no one ever sent me yet one perfect
limousine, do you suppose? Ah no, it's always
just my luck to get one perfect rose.

Dorothy Parker, born 8/22/1893

It would have been a helluva lot more fun
if I had not hit those 61 home runs.

Roger Maris, born 9/10/1934

They all want me to continue being the great mountain
climber, in good condition and pursuing great
adventures; yet they also want me to be sitting in their
offices, cutting films or writing articles and books.

Reinhold Messner, born 9/17/1944

It worries me a little bit the reach and power of TV. More people saw me in The Practice than will ever see me in all the stage plays I ever do. Which is sort of humbling. Or troubling. Or both.

Michael Emerson, born 9/7/1954

I'm doing one more year. After that, we'll wait and see. It's tough. The show is getting more popular, which isn't the way it's really supposed to work. You're supposed to peak your second year, coast in your third and fourth, and split. It doesn't seem to be working out that way.

Jason Priestley, born 8/28/1969,
whining about 90210's success

As far as, you know, actually doing it every night, it's pretty much a pain, wearing that fat suit and talking in that high voice for hours.

Tyler Perry, born 9/13/1969,
about playing his character Madea on stage

To be honest, I feel people would have acknowledged my talent a lot more.

Beyoncé, born 9/4/1981,
about if she hadn't been beautiful

Criticism

When not complaining, the Virgo tongue criticizes. Virgo promptly passes judgment and offers advice. Your critical nature extends to yourself, too. You're quick to chastise yourself for inadequacy and imperfection.

You may scold a carpenter who has made you a bad table, though you cannot make a table. It is not your trade to make tables.

Samuel Johnson, born 9/18/1709

It is much easier to recognize error than to find truth; error is superficial and may be corrected; truth lies hidden in the depths.

Goethe, born 8/28/1749

It is easier to discover a deficiency in individuals, in states, and in Providence, than to see their real import and value.

Georg Hegel, born 8/27/1770

Everyone thinks of changing the world, but no one thinks of changing himself.

Leo Tolstoy, born 9/9/1828

No passion in the world is equal to the passion to alter someone else's draft.

H.G. Wells, born 9/21/1866

To the Puritan all things are impure, as somebody says.

D.H. Lawrence, born 9/11/1885
Etruscan Places

I am patient with stupidity, but not with those who are proud of it.

Edith Sitwell, born 9/7/1887

If one sticks too rigidly to one's principles, one would hardly see anybody.

Agatha Christie, born 9/15/1890

Runs the gamut of emotions from A to B.

Dorothy Parker, born 8/22/1893
Theater review

The first question I ask myself when something doesn't seem to be beautiful is why do I think it's not beautiful. And very shortly you discover that there is no reason.

John Cage, born 9/5/1912

If ignorance is bliss, why aren't there more happy people in the world?

Stephen Fry, born 8/24/1957

You can tell how much thought a person put into a gift by the wrapping.

Faith Ford, born 9/14/1964

If we had no faults of our own, we should take less pleasure in noticing the faults of others.

François de La Rochefoucauld, born 9/15/1613

What I have done, anyone could have done. I haven't any special attainments.

J.C. Penney, born 9/16/1875

No man of honor ever quite lives up to his code, any more than a moral man manages to avoid sin.

H.L. Mencken, born 9/12/1880

I can't write five words but that I change seven.

Dorothy Parker, born 8/22/1893

To say something nice about themselves—this is the hardest thing in the world for people to do. They'd rather take their clothes off.

Nancy Friday, born 8/27/1933

I watch other actors and think, "That's a proper actor—I'm a plumber, really."

Jeremy Irons, born 9/19/1948

Sometimes I can be my own worst critic.

Reggie Miller, born 8/24/1965

I don't spend money on myself. I don't like myself yet.

Adam Sandler, born 9/9/1966

There's a voice inside each one of our heads, very strong in my head, which is really critical, and it's "You know, you're not good enough."

David Arquette, born 9/8/1971

My ego still drives me—I'm still insecure about dumb things. But I'm aware of it and I work on it. At least that's something!

Michael Bublé, born 9/9/1975

Crassness

More than other signs of the zodiac, Virgo surprises with rough-edged vulgarity. Actress Melissa Leo (9/14/1960) used the F word in her Oscar acceptance speech to become one of the few winners ever bleeped during TV broadcasts. Baseball coach Tommy Lasorda (9/22/1927) had to make frequent apologies for his on-field swearing. Writer Karrine Steffans (8/24/1978) chooses book titles like *Confessions of a Video Vixen* and *Drink F--- Sleep*.

If all the girls attending the Yale Prom were laid end to end, I wouldn't be at all surprised.

Dorothy Parker, born 8/22/1893

I never trust a man unless I've got
his pecker in my pocket.

Lyndon Johnson, born 8/27/1908

There's people making babies to my music. That's nice.

Barry White, born 9/12/1944

Looking like a man who just came out of the crapper
and can't quite remember if he's wiped himself . . .

Stephen King, born 9/21/1947
Needful Things

His court pantomimes are invariably sexual, his imprecations obscene, his attempts at comedy and his belligerent statements sexual or scatological . . . Jimbo was going to show the world that he is not some sissy or mama's boy, but that he can be as coarse and crude as any father's son.

about Jimmy Connors, born 9/2/1952
Sports Illustrated

Basically, for the first 24 hours you have
to sniff each other like dogs.

Amy Poehler, born 9/16/1971

That's the song I lost my virginity to!

Cameron Diaz, born 8/30/1972,
interrupting an interview

I need my nipples squeezed before every
show. It gets me pumped to go onstage. My
assistant Jackie has it down to a fine art.

Pink, born 9/8/1979

When I was younger, I felt the weight of everything on my shoulders without the promise of anything. I was messier. A lot of that came out of embarrassment, just mortification. And after the things my body has just accomplished, I don't feel as guilty or apologetic. It was all because of the pregnancy. Well, more so the delivery. Sorry, I'm naked! Sorry I'm bleeding! Sorry I'm pooping! None of that! I'm not sorry!

Michelle Williams, born 9/9/1980

At Home

- **Shy Child**
- **Helpful Sibling**
- **Instructive Parent**
- **Sensible Budget**
- **Careful Appearance**
- **Neat House**
- **Healthy Eater**

Shy Child

The shy Virgo child tries to hide. Your struggle to integrate with the outside world proves most difficult in your early years. Each Virgo needs introspection before opening up.

Your world is as big as you make it.
I know, for I used to abide
In the narrowest nest in a corner,
My wings pressing close to my side.

Georgia Douglas Johnson, born 9/10/1880

Why is there such an innate demand
for secrecy in a child's mind?

Agatha Christie, born 9/15/1890

I was the shyest human being ever invented. I couldn't come into a room without bumping into the furniture and then blushing. If people asked me what my name was, I'd blush bright scarlet. At school, I knew the answers to many of the questions but I'd never answer them because as soon as I was on my feet I'd go a deep crimson and start to stammer.

Ingrid Bergman, born 8/29/1915

I was kind of a shy kid. I've developed
into a bit of a talker since then.

Ted Williams, born 8/30/1918

Sometimes I would go around the corner and hide so
deep in another apartment house's basement that by
the time I came out, people weren't playing anymore.

Elliott Gould, born 8/29/1938

I was very shy. I mean, I'm an introvert
in life and an extrovert on stage.

Swoosie Kurtz, born 9/6/1944,
about being the new kid in grade school

I grew up belonging to the low self-esteem
club, never feeling pretty and afraid men
would find a smart woman intimidating.

Jacqueline Bisset, born 9/13/1944

I used to be very private and secretive. Now
I've opened up the dark corners of my life.

Peggy Lipton, born 8/30/1946

I used to be so withdrawn. I had to be to survive. But inside I was like a volcano.

Gloria Estefan, born 9/1/1957

I had pimples so badly it used to make me so shy. I used not to look at myself. I'd hide my face in the dark, I wouldn't want to look in the mirror and my father teased me and I just hated it and I cried everyday.

Michael Jackson, born 8/29/1958

I didn't have a boyfriend until I was 17. There were boys at school that I would find out later had a crush on me but I was too shy to talk to them.

Blake Lively, born 8/25/1987

Helpful Sibling

Virgo is the most frequent Sun sign in famous entertainment families. Virgo strengthens the team by putting the group first. In either starring or secondary roles, Virgo provides a practical glue that helps sustain the family unit.

Virgo Specialty: Steady Presence in Famous Families

Family	Field	Virgo Representative	Birthdate
Thompson	Reality TV	Honey Boo Boo	8/28/2005
Jonas	Music	Nick Jonas	9/16/1992
Windsor	Royalty	Prince Harry	9/15/1984
Culkin	Acting	Macaulay Culkin	8/26/1980
Hudson / Hawn	Acting	Oliver Hudson	9/7/1976
Wilson	Acting	Luke Wilson	9/21/1971
Smith	Acting, music	Jada Pinkett Smith	9/18/1971
Arquette	Acting	David Arquette	9/8/1971
Sheen / Estevez	Acting	Charlie Sheen	9/3/1965
Wayans	Entertainment	Damon Wayans	9/4/1960

Marsalis	Music	Branford Marsalis	8/26/1960
Jackson	Music	Michael Jackson	8/29/1958
Gibb	Music	Barry Gibb	9/1/1946

Politeness, that cementer of friendship and soother of enmities, is nowhere so much required, and so frequently outraged, as in family circles.

Marguerite Blessington, born 9/1/1789
The Repealers

Peace and war start within one's own home. If we really want peace for the world, let us start by loving one another within our families. Sometimes it is hard for us to smile at one another.

Mother Teresa, born 8/26/1910

One of the biggest problems of the modern household is that it isn't private anymore. People don't even understand the concept—they equate privacy with shame. As a result, they will gossip as freely about their families and friends as they would about strangers. Sacrificing the dignity of your intimates by going public does not have a soothing effect on family life. There should be such a thing as loyalty.

Judith Martin, born 9/13/1938

I love my family very much. I wish I could see them a little more often than I do. But we understand because we're a show business family and we all work.

Michael Jackson, born 8/29/1958

Dad kept us out of school, but school comes and goes. Family is forever.

Charlie Sheen, born 9/3/1965

I have three nieces and a nephew. I know what it's like. I've changed the diapers. I've seen three births, so I totally get the whole picture.

Cameron Diaz, born 8/30/1972

It's a bit startling to achieve global recognition before the age of 30 on account of your sister, your brother-in-law and your bottom.

Pippa Middleton, born 9/6/1983

I will always give him as much support as I can.

Prince Harry, born 9/15/1984,
about Cancer brother Prince William

We make decisions together—even when we're doing things individually.

Nick Jonas, born 9/16/1992

Instructive Parent

When you parent, you teach. Virgo cultivates discipline and instills the importance of hard work. Patriarch Joseph Kennedy (9/6/1888) impressed the public service and prestige of his U.S. ambassadorship upon his descendants. Judith Martin (9/13/1938) contributed a series of etiquette guidebooks under the pen name Miss Manners. Instead of enriching his children, Warren Buffett (8/30/1930) plans charitable donation for the bulk of his estate.

They've all gone their own ways to accomplish a lot. They're productive, and they don't expect to just be some rich guy's kid.

Warren Buffett, born 8/30/1930,
about his three children

Children generally hate to be idle. All the care then should be, that their busy humor should be constantly employed in something that is of use to them.

John Locke, born 8/29/1632

Loving a child doesn't mean giving in to all his whims; to love him is to bring out the best in him, to teach him to love what is difficult.

Nadia Boulanger, born 9/16/1887

People should tell their children what life is all about—it's about work.

Lauren Bacall, born 9/16/1924

We are all born charming, fresh, and spontaneous and must be civilized before we are fit to participate in society.

Judith Martin, born 9/13/1938
Miss Manners' Guide to Excruciatingly Correct Behavior

The dinner table is the center for the teaching and practicing not just of table manners but of conversation, consideration, tolerance, family feeling, and just about all the other accomplishments of polite society except the minuet.

Judith Martin, born 9/13/1938
Miss Manners' Guide for the Turn-of-the-Millennium

Your job is to cherish your children, protect them, and prepare them for the world.

Phil McGraw, born 9/1/1950

As a parent, I've found out that kids don't want "quality time" with you. They want "quantity." In fact, they want all of your time. Of course, they need interaction and communication, but just your presence there in the house means the world to them.

I asked my girls, "Would you rather see me once a week and we go to Disneyland, or would you rather just have me here every night?" And they said, "Every night."

Jeff Foxworthy, born 9/6/1958

I've asked her not to do her booty shake at school. Somehow she's learned to shake it in a Beyoncé sort of way. I don't want her to rein it in entirely, but I'd like her to use a little discretion; choose the right time and place!

Actress Cheryl Hines, born 9/21/1965

It's my most important job. I have them for half the week. I cook all their meals, take them to school and do their homework with them. But I miss making ponytails and tying their shoes.

Louie C.K., born 9/12/1967

Parenting is 90% energy; if you don't have it, then there tend to be some lazy TV-watching days with the kids, and that ain't gettin' it done. A great day with them—my sons are 4 and 2—is an energized adventure into the world.

Jack Black, born 8/28/1969

I like boundaries. We didn't have many. I think structure is good for kids. I want to make sure Coco is very nerdy for a long time.

David Arquette, born 9/8/1971

Sensible Budget

Aries buys impulsively, Sagittarius spends indiscriminately, and Leo and Capricorn use money to show off. Virgo stays practical. You spend for necessities, shop for bargains, and save for the next rainy day.

Whatever you have, spend less.
Samuel Johnson, born 9/18/1709

Put not your trust in money, but
put your money in trust.
Oliver Wendell Holmes, born 8/29/1809
The Autocrat of the Breakfast Table

Where large sums of money are concerned,
it is advisable to trust nobody.
Agatha Christie, born 9/15/1890

You only have to do a very few things right in your
life—so long as you don't do too many things wrong.
Warren Buffett, born 8/30/1930

When you can buy classic penny tile for 99 cents a sheet for your bathroom, it doesn't make sense to spend $70 per square foot on hand-painted tile. If you want to experiment in those spaces, do so through paint and the color of towels and accessories.
Nate Berkus, born 9/17/1971

You don't have to pay a million dollars
for clothes that look good.
Rachel Bilson, born 8/25/1981

You can't beat the price. Free is in my budget.
Golfer Brittany Lincicome, born 9/19/1985

I think it's better to buy real estate than,
say, a yellow and purple corvette or an
elephant that can speak sign language.
Shaun White, born 9/3/1986

Usually I'm quite sensible with my [money].

Rupert Grint, born 8/24/1988

Careful Appearance

Virgo's interest in detail comes through in fussy clothes. You like ribbons, frills and accessories. Country singer George Jones (9/12/1931) had an in-house barber fix his hair every day. Contemporary celebrities Rachel Bilson (8/25/1981), Nicole Richie (9/21/1981) and Lea Michele (8/29/1986) are never seen with even a hair out of place. Virgo feels best when perfectly groomed.

She plucked from my lapel the invisible strand of lint (the universal act of woman to proclaim ownership).

O. Henry, born 9/11/1862
A Ramble in Aphasia

He was dressed in a wine-colored smoking jacket, just as natty as you please, and not a hair out of place.

Stephen King, born 9/21/1947
Needful Things

I admit it. I take care of myself, and I enjoy it.

Football star Jason Taylor, born 9/1/1974,
about getting manicures and pedicures

When I've just gotten out of the shower. I'm clean and I have on nice lingerie and I'm getting in the bed—I feel really beautiful then.

Beyoncé, born 9/4/1981,
about when she feels most beautiful

I love to mix things up. I love using basics as a canvas, combining them with vintage pieces or piling on accessories.

Rachel Bilson, born 8/25/1981

Accessories speak volumes, especially when dressed down in jeans.
Nicole Richie, born 9/21/1981

I love the little details like the flowers in front.
Florence Welch, born 8/28/1986

I'm buying all these vintage brooches to use as hair ornaments, decoration, everything.
Emmy Rossum, born 9/12/1986

I liked it because it's sparkly and fluffy.
Quvenzhané Wallis, born 8/28/2003,
about her Oscar dress

Neat House

I'm a Virgo, so I am very organized and I am very obsessive about neatness.
Charlie Sheen, born 9/3/1965

Yes, you can be obsessively tidy. You insist that your immediate surroundings stay neat and organized. Screen legend Greta Garbo (9/18/1905) scrubbed her own front steps at home in New York City. Fellow superstars Ingrid Bergman (8/29/1915) and Sophia Loren (9/20/1934) mastered household chores. Routine cleaning settles the anxious Virgo mind.

Would they had swept cleaner!—
Here's a littering shred
Of linen left behind—a vile reproach
To all good housewifery.
Lydia Howard Sigourney, born 9/1/1791

It's too long a story to tell over greasy plates.

H.G. Wells, born 9/21/1866
The Time Machine

I got the blues thinking of the future, so I left off and made some marmalade. It's amazing how it cheers one up to shred oranges and scrub the floor.

D.H. Lawrence, born 9/11/1885

The best time for planning a book is while you're doing the dishes.

Agatha Christie, born 9/15/1890

Excuse my dust.

Dorothy Parker, born 8/22/1893
Epitaph for herself

But housework I was very good at. The scrubbing and cleaning of a house or apartment from top to bottom has always satisfied my Scandinavian soul. One of my friends always said, "How you've wasted all these years being an actress when you could have been the best charwoman in the business."

Ingrid Bergman, born 8/29/1915

I like to keep [my lawn] real manicured. By the time you finish, it's time to start mowing again.

George Jones, born 9/12/1931

Joy has never—and this is very rare for a housewife—never picked up a pair of my shoes! Never had to!

Regis Philbin, born 8/25/1931

We are not afraid to look under the bed, or to wash the sheets; we know that life is messy. We know that somebody has to clean it up, and that only if it is cleaned up can we hope to start over, and get better.

Marsha Norman, 9/21/1947

I'm textbook OCD. I love to clean.

Ed Begley Jr., born 9/16/1949

On a really awesome day, I'll spend the afternoon cleaning out my closets. I love to organize.

Amy Poehler, born 9/16/1971

Clean your house, people. It costs nothing.

Nate Berkus, born 9/17/1971,
his #1 tip to improve home decor

Washing my cars.

Baseball player José Vidro, born 8/27/1974,
about his favorite off-day activity

Poirot completed his packing—a very simple affair, since his possessions were always in the most meticulous order.

Agatha Christie, born 9/15/1890
Death on the Nile

It's not the tragedies that kill us, it's the messes. I can't stand messes.

Dorothy Parker, born 8/22/1893

I'm absolutely obsessed with orderliness. I can't live in a house where there is disorder; I become absolutely ill.

Ingrid Bergman, born 8/29/1915

There's a difference between a nice arrangement of things and a mess, and it's called clutter.

David Arquette, born 9/8/1971

I've got Band-Aids, Neosporin, anything they need. I'm really organized!

Brooke Burke, born 9/8/1971,
about what's in her purse

Don't keep a messy house. If you meet someone tomorrow, don't you want to be able to bring her home?

Ludacris, born 9/11/1977

I love home décor—I'm obsessed. I'm a big flea market person. I'm into amazing antiques and even eBay, and I also love Anthropologie. They have the cutest salt and pepper shakers and a sugar bowl with a little bird sitting on it. They just have the nicest knickknacks.

Rachel Bilson, born 8/25/1981

I'm one of those people who has to have everything in the right spot or else I feel like it's going to be all wrong.

Nick Jonas, born 9/16/1992

Healthy Eater

As the zodiac's most health-conscious sign, Virgo ingests with care. Thomas Tryon (9/6/1634) wrote 17th-century self-help books advocating vegetarianism. Virgo claims a relatively high number of famous vegetarians including Mary Shelley (8/30/1797), Leo Tolstoy (9/9/1828) and Shania Twain (8/28/1965). Virgo stays aware of what you eat.

A meal of bread, cheese, and beer
constitutes the perfect food.
Queen Elizabeth I, born 9/17/1533

I'm really a gardener. Not so much flowers as edibles. Because of movies and the series schedule, the only thing I've planted this year is lettuce. But this summer, I'll put in corn and tomatoes.
Jean Smart, born 9/13/1951

Look a cow in the eye before eating a hamburger.
Moby, born 9/11/1965

My book came from years of trying to get my own children to eat healthy foods—my own trial and error in my own kitchen. The idea of pureeing vegetables has been around for decades.
Jessica Seinfeld, born 9/12/1971

I buy only what I need for the week and get super creative with leftovers. It's so satisfying to use everything in the fridge before it goes to waste.
Cameron Diaz, born 8/30/1972

I have to be in shape to fit into those little costumes so I eat vegetables and fish—and Special K. I hate water, so I always ask for cucumber and lemons, because I drink water with them. That's my diva demand.
Beyoncé, born 9/4/1981

But the gift that I wanted was the nutrition facts . . . Now I know that the caramel popcorn is four points a cup while the cheese popcorn is five; I know exactly what I'm putting in my body. And that makes me so happy!

Jennifer Hudson, born 9/12/1981

I eat fruits, vegetables, lean meats and limit
refined carbs like white flour. I'll have three or four
bites of something I love, like mac and cheese,
and I'm good. I don't need a batch of it.

LeAnn Rimes, born 8/28/1982

I'm a vegan, and that has always helped me.

Lea Michele, born 8/29/1986

Relationships

- **I Just Want to be Alone**
- **Slow to Intimacy**
- **Conscious of Mating**
- **Helpful Friend**

I Just Want to be Alone

Nicknamed "the Virgin Queen," England's Elizabeth I (9/17/1933) steadfastly refused to marry throughout her 44-year reign. "I just want to be alone," said legendary actress Greta Garbo (9/18/1905) both on and off the screen. To remain self-sufficient and bypass the obligation to compromise, Virgo resists engaging with other people. Many Virgos choose single life over a domestic partnership.

> *And to me it shall be a full satisfaction both for the Memorial of my name, and for my glory also, if when I shall let my last breath, it be engraven upon my Marble Tomb, Here lyeth ELIZABETH, which reigned a Virgin, and died a Virgin.*
>
> Queen Elizabeth I, born 9/17/1533

I would rather be a beggar and single, than a Queen and married . . . I should call the wedding ring the yoke ring.

Queen Elizabeth I, born 9/17/1533

I was always an independent, even when I had partners.

Samuel Goldwyn, born 8/27/1882

You love me so much, you want to put me in your pocket. And I should die there smothered.

D.H. Lawrence, born 9/11/1885

Marriage is like paying an endless visit in your worst clothes.

J.B. Priestley, born 9/13/1894

I've never minded being on my own. It was my choice.

Greta Garbo, born 9/18/1905

I haven't been in a relationship for like five years now, It was so hard the last time . . . It was just like, "Aggh! God, forget all that, man, let's just be friends."

Keanu Reeves, born 9/2/1964

I have seen nothing to recommend marriage.

Keanu Reeves, born 9/2/1964

I really didn't ever want to love again after the end of my marriage. I decided I could live the rest of my life without love, but I was wrong. And I'm so glad I was wrong.

Shania Twain, born 8/28/1965

The first 28 years of my life, it was hell and misery. Now I can do whatever I want. I don't want any drama; I don't want to argue; I don't want to answer to anybody. I've worked too hard to get here, and I'm loving this freedom.

Tyler Perry, born 9/13/1969

Sometimes, in relationships, the pleasure is all theirs. Alone, I am a superhero. With you, I am a mere mortal. You deplete me. I'm tired of being your upgrade. We are not equally yoked. You really deserve someone more basic. I'm tired of pretending your mediocracy is okay with me.

Karrine Steffans, born 8/24/1978

I never really believed in marriage and I still don't somewhat, but I also believe you can make things your own.

Pink, born 9/8/1979

Slow to Intimacy

Virgo maintains multiple layers of self-protection. You resist the formal definition of a relationship, then wrestle with physical intimacy. Virgo holds something in reserve.

It took me nine years to get married, ten to become an actor.

Peter Falk, born 9/16/1927

[Director] Richard Curtis really believes that people can fall in love, do fall in love. Oddly, people like me find it quite hard.

Hugh Grant, born 9/9/1960

They're going to have to pursue me like I'm the queen in order to get a date because I'm worth it, damn it. I'm a catch.

Virginia Madsen, born 9/11/1961

I think that what I've found, in my experience, is that you always find the person who you're meant to be with at that time in your life. And what I've also found is that you have to move on from those people at certain times, because that's the way it happens.

Cameron Diaz, born 8/30/1972

I want to get married, but I'm always tortured in relationships. There are six billion people in the world. It's hard to find the one person who's right for you.

Scott Caan, born 8/23/1976

Don't throw yourself at a woman on the first date no matter how beautiful or fabulous she is . . . and you shouldn't share your whole life story within the first hour 'cause what will you talk about next?

Ludacris, born 9/11/1977

I had a girlfriend for about four years, and it just stopped working after a while. I don't know. It's tough now to meet a girl who wants to hang out with you because she likes your personality—who hasn't seen you on TV and is like "Hey."

Shaun White, born 9/3/1986

I'm very old-fashioned in terms of my values. I'm old-fashioned about relationships—how quickly they move—and about loyalty.

Emmy Rossum, born 9/12/1986

They perceived that the love, unceasing and ecstatic, of which they had dreamt before their union, was a chimera existing only in imagination; and they awoke, with sobered feelings, to seek content in rational affection, instead of indulging in romantic expectations that never fall to the lot of human beings: each acknowledging, with a sigh, that even in a marriage of love, the brilliant anticipations of imagination are never realized; that disappointment awaits poor mortals even in that brightest portion of existence—The Honey-Moon.

Marguerite Blessington, born 9/1/1789
The Honey-Moon

As soon as he had lifted her in his arms, she wanted to scream to him not to touch her. She stiffened herself . . . She had never, never wanted to be given over to this. But she had willed that it should happen to her. And according to her will, she lay and let it happen. But she never wanted it. She never wanted to be thus assailed and handled and mauled. She wanted to keep herself to herself . . . She panted with relief when it was over.

D.H. Lawrence, born 9/11/1885
The Princess

It's always been a pet peeve of mine if a guy is like, "So is it okay if I kiss you now?" It's so much cooler to just go for it as opposed to announcing it and ruining the moment. It's like saying, "Let's talk about this: My lips are going to go here at a 90-degree angle—how do you feel about that?"

Rachel Bilson, born 8/25/1981

In the life of each of us, I said to myself, there
is a place remote and islanded, and given
to endless regret or secret happiness.

Sarah Orne Jewett, born 9/3/1849
The Country of the Pointed Firs

They wanted genuine intimacy, but they could not get even normally near to anyone, because they scorned to take the first steps, they scorned the triviality which forms common human intercourse.

D.H. Lawrence, born 9/11/1885

For there is always a sanctuary more, a door that can never be forced, whatever the force, a last invincible stronghold that can never be taken, whatever the attack; your vote can be taken, your name, your innards, even your life, but that last stronghold can only be surrendered. And to surrender it for any reason other than love is to surrender love.

Ken Kesey, born 9/17/1935

It's a pleasure to have your preconceptions about a person proved wrong. Pie in the face with no downside.

Bill Murray, born 9/21/1950

Conscious of Mating

Ever cognizant of bodily functions, you think about the physical coupling component of one-on-one relationships. Virgo refers to the mating process more readily than other zodiac signs.

For the butterfly, mating and propagation involve the sacrifice of life; for the human being, the sacrifice of beauty.

Goethe, born 8/28/1749

The real hope of the world lies in putting as painstaking thought into the business of mating as we do into other big businesses.

Margaret Sanger, born 9/14/1883

A man and a woman need each other's DNA and hence can enjoy sex. A man and a woman have a common interest in their children and their enduring love has evolved to protect that interest. And a husband and wife can be each other's best friends, and can enjoy the lifelong dependability and trust that underlies the logic of friendship. These emotions are rooted in the fact that if a man and woman are monogamous, together for life . . . their genetic interests are identical.

Steven Pinker, born 9/18/1954
How the Mind Works

Helpful Friend

Virgo may struggle with romantic relationships, but your helpfulness makes you a good friend. You listen, evaluate, advise and encourage. Virgo's consistent support breeds long-lasting friendships.

A true friend is the greatest of all blessings, and that which we take the least care of all to acquire.

François de La Rochefoucauld, born 9/15/1613

We cannot tell the precise moment when friendship is formed. As in filling a vessel drop by drop, there is at last a drop which makes it run over; so in a series of kindnesses there is at last one which makes the heart run over.

Samuel Johnson, born 9/18/1709

Don't flatter yourself that friendship authorizes you to say disagreeable things to your intimates. The nearer you come into relation with a person, the more necessary do tact and courtesy become.

Oliver Wendell Holmes, born 8/29/1809

The growth of true friendship may be a lifelong affair.
Sarah Orne Jewett, born 9/3/1849

You can always tell a real friend: When you make a fool of yourself, he doesn't feel you've done a permanent job.
Laurence Peter, born 9/16/1919

After all, how many good friends can you have in life? Four or five. The rest are just acquaintances you meet at a party.
Sophia Loren, born 9/20/1934

Friends don't spy; true friendship is about privacy, too.
Stephen King, born 9/21/1947
Hearts in Atlantis

I'm not really here to shop. Sari [Gueron] is a friend. Philip [Limm] is a friend. They've been supportive of me. And if this is what it means for me to be supportive of them, I'm happy to do it.
Michelle Williams, born 9/9/1980,
attending fashion show

I'm a girl's girl. Women who don't have female friends scare me.
Beyoncé, born 9/4/1981

Famous Virgo Relationships

Romantic compatibility is the most popular area of astrological inquiry and one of the most complex. The Sun-sign relationship describing the core energy flow between two individuals is based on each sign's traits and on relative location within the zodiac circle. Here are astrology's traditional assessments of Virgo's compatibility with other zodiac signs:

Virgo's Partner	Usual Dates	Energy Flow	Relation to Virgo on the Zodiac Circle
Sagittarius	Nov. 23 through Dec. 21	Challenging	Square (90 degrees)
Gemini	May 21 through Jun. 20	Challenging	Square (90 degrees)
Virgo	Aug. 23 through Sept. 21	Challenging	None (0 degrees)
Aquarius	Jan. 20 through Feb. 18	Neutral	Weak (150 degrees)
Aries	Mar. 21 through Apr. 19	Neutral	Weak (150 degrees)
Libra	Sept. 22 through Oct. 22	Positive	Adjacent (30 degrees)
Leo	Jul. 22 through Aug. 22	Positive	Adjacent (30 degrees)
Scorpio	Oct. 23 through Nov. 22	Positive	Sextile (60 degrees)
Cancer	Jun. 21 through Jul. 21	Positive	Sextile (60 degrees)
Capricorn	Dec. 22 through Jan. 19	Very Positive	Triangle (120 degrees)
Taurus	Apr. 20 through May 20	Very Positive	Triangle (120 degrees)
Pisces	Feb. 19 through Mar. 20	Very Positive	Opposite (180 degrees)

Certain Sun placements are more likely to generate mutually beneficial relationships with Virgo. But the following tables demonstrate that Virgo forms both successful and unsuccessful relationships with individuals from each zodiac sign. Sun signs tell only part of the story indicated by a full comparison of individual birth charts. The zodiac sign of each individual's Moon and the interaction of the planets also impact the relationship. One person's astrological talents and challenges can complement, antagonize or have little impact on another person's natural tendencies. Visit a qualified astrologer for additional insight into your relationship potential. For a list of recommended astrologers, go to www.QuotableZodiac.com.

Astrology indicates tendencies, but individuals still exercise free will within relationships. There are no quick answers to getting along well with someone else. Astrological awareness can help two individuals blend their natural characteristics to mutual advantage.

Challenging: Virgo with Sagittarius

Virgo prefers a clean, neat environment but the Sagittarian's many interests collect clutter. Virgo's very specific advice tries to be helpful but instead dampens the Sagittarian's freewheeling enthusiasm.

The following supposedly difficult pairings include some well-known, long-lasting relationships. To all appearances, Virgos Beyoncé and Amy Madigan enjoy committed relationships with Sagittarian partners. As within an individual's birth-chart, great strength comes from overcoming the tension of the square.

Virgo	Birthdate	Sagittarius	Relationship
Nick Jonas	9/16/1992	Miley Cyrus	Girlfriend, split
LeAnn Rimes	8/28/1982	Dean Sheremet	Spouse, divorced
Beyoncé	9/4/1981	Jay-Z	Spouse
Rachel Bilson	8/25/1981	Adam Brody	Boyfriend, split
Marlee Matlin	8/24/1965	Jennifer Beals	Good friend
Billy Ray Cyrus	8/25/1961	Miley Cyrus	Daughter
Ethan Coen	9/21/1957	Joel Coen	Brother, co-director
Jimmy Connors	9/2/1952	Chris Evert	Fiancée, split
Amy Madigan	9/11/1950	Ed Harris	Spouse
Sophia Loren	9/20/1934	Carlo Ponti	Spouse
Margaret Taylor	9/21/1788	Zachary Taylor	Spouse
Louis XIV (France)	9/5/1638	Madame de Maintenon	Mistress, then wife
Elizabeth I (England)	9/17/1533	Mary Queen of Scots	Royal rival

Milton was a genius that could cut a Colossus from a rock; but he could not carve heads upon cherrystones.

Samuel Johnson, born 9/18/1709,
about Sagittarius John Milton

Don't even dream of patronizing her because of her age. She will voice her opinion in no uncertain terms.

Colin Firth, born 9/10/1960,
about Sagittarian costar Scarlett Johansson

Challenging: Virgo with Gemini

Nervous energy galore! Virgo Sun-sign individuals are challenged by the 90-degree square relationship with Gemini. The brittle Virgo-Gemini pairing links two high-strung individuals tinkering nonstop with the immediate environment. Virgo worries, Gemini talks, both meddle. The combination delivers so much surface activity that development of a firm foundation can fall by the wayside.

Virgo	Birthdate	Gemini	Relationship
LeAnn Rimes	8/28/1982	Eddie Cibrian	Spouse
Macaulay Culkin	8/26/1980	Natalie Portman	Close friend
David Arquette	9/8/1971	Courteney Cox	Spouse, divorced
Padma Lakshmi	9/1/1970	Salman Rushdie	Spouse, divorced
Salma Hayek	9/2/1966	François-Henri Pinault	Spouse
Hugh Grant	9/9/1960	Elizabeth Hurley	Lover, split
Tim Burton	8/25/1958	Helena Bonham Carter	Domestic partner
Anne Meara	9/20/1929	Jerry Stiller	Spouse, comedy partner
Alan Jay Lerner	8/31/1918	Frederick Loewe	Songwriting partner
Clayton Moore	9/14/1914	Jay Silverheels	Lone Ranger costar
William Taft	9/15/1857	Helen Herren Taft	Spouse
Clara Schumann	9/13/1819	Robert Schumann	Spouse
Prince Albert	8/26/1819	Queen Victoria	Spouse

I am a housewife. I cook every night for my husband. He's a spoiled brat when it comes to food.

Salma Hayek

Challenging: Virgo with Virgo

The most successful same-sign relationships seem to be Libra with Libra, where each person's constant balancing and reflection of the other person keeps the focus on the partnership. But most relationships with the same Sun sign bring together too much of the same personality traits. Virgo with Virgo brings organized space and a mutual interest in helping others. But Virgos can nitpick each other. You must guard against isolating yourselves and worrying too much about minor issues. The Virgo-Virgo combination lacks the contrast that forces relationship growth.

Virgo	Birthdate	Virgo	Birthdate	Relationship
Blake Lively	8/25/1987	Florence Welch	8/28/1986	Close friend
Alex O'Loughlin	8/24/1976	Scott Caan	8/23/1976	TV costar
Claudia Schiffer	8/25/1970	David Copperfield	9/16/1956	Fiancé, split
Mike Piazza	9/4/1968	Tommy Lasorda	9/22/1927	Mentor, coach
Michael Jackson	8/29/1958	Macaulay Culkin	8/26/1980	Friend
John Ritter	9/17/1948	Amy Yasbeck	9/12/1962	Spouse
Louis Teicher	8/24/1924	Arthur Ferrante	9/7/1921	Piano partner
Louis XIV (France)	9/5/1638	Colbert	8/29/1619	22-yr. finance minister

He's the best kisser I've ever met. He also throws his socks in the hamper. What more do you want?

Amy Yasbeck about John Ritter

Neutral: Virgo with Aquarius

The Virgo Sun is 150 degrees of the zodiac away from Aquarius, making a weak connection if any. The two signs move along different wavelengths. Virgo's social and sexual reserve doesn't mesh with Aquarian curiosity and experimentation. Virgo gladly helps specific individuals; Aquarius avoids personal connection while supporting the humanitarian cause. The storybook marriage of Virgo Lauren Bacall and Aquarius Humphrey Bogart underscores that, like all signs, Virgo can form satisfying relationships with any sign of the

zodiac. But elements other than the Sun signs generally hold these relationships together.

Virgo	Birthdate	Aquarius	Relationship
Nicole Richie	9/21/1981	Paris Hilton	Off-and-on friend
Cameron Diaz	8/30/1972	Justin Timberlake	Lover, split
Lance Armstrong	9/18/1971	Sheryl Crow	Lover, split
Queen Rania	8/31/1970	King Abdullah (Jordan)	Spouse
Charlie Sheen	9/3/1965	Denise Richards	Spouse, divorced
Trisha Yearwood	9/19/1964	Garth Brooks	Collaborator, spouse
Michael Jackson	8/29/1958	Lisa Marie Presley	Spouse, divorced
Richard Gere	8/31/1949	Carey Lowell	Spouse
Richard Gere	8/31/1949	Diane Lane	Movie costar (3x)
Jeremy Irons	9/19/1948	Sinead Cusack	Spouse
Regis Philbin	8/25/1931	Joy Philbin	Spouse
Arnold Palmer	9/10/1929	Jack Nicklaus	Golf rival; friend
Lauren Bacall	9/16/1924	Humphrey Bogart	Costar, spouse
Brant Parker	8/26/1920	Johnny Hart	Cartoon collaborator
Ingrid Bergman	8/29/1915	Humphrey Bogart	Movie costar

She's smart, funny and really quirky. She's a goofball—who likes goofballs—which is great because I'm a goofball.

Richard Gere about Carey Lowell

He's got that old-fashioned manly quality, which is very attractive. And he's a very open-minded kind of guy.

Queen Rania about King Abdullah

Neutral: Virgo with Aries

The Virgo Sun is 150 degrees of the zodiac circle away from Aries, making a weak connection if any. The Virgo and Aries individuals have different styles—Aries the free and uncensored Casanova, Virgo the modest and discriminating maiden. Virgo's

careful attention to detail doesn't mesh with Aries haste and recklessness. Aries' disdain for outside opinion upsets Virgo's preference for good manners. Elements other than the Sun signs generally hold Virgo-Aries relationships together.

Virgo	Birthdate	Aries	Relationship
Andy Roddick	8/30/1982	Brooklyn Decker	Spouse
Andy Roddick	8/30/1982	Mandy Moore	Lover, split
Nicole Richie	9/21/1981	DJ AM	Fiancé, split
Jennifer Hudson	9/12/1981	David Otunga	Fiancé
Rachel Bilson	8/25/1981	Hayden Christensen	Lover
Michelle Williams	9/9/1980	Heath Ledger	Domestic partner, split
Ryan Phillippe	9/10/1974	Reese Witherspoon	Spouse, divorced
Harry Connick Jr.	9/11/1967	Jill Goodacre	Spouse
Charlie Sheen	9/3/1965	Jon Cryer	TV comedy costar
Conway Twitty	9/1/1933	Loretta Lynn	Music collaborator
Oliver Lynn	8/27/1926	Loretta Lynn	Spouse
Charles Rolls	8/27/1877	Frederick Royce	Rolls-Royce cofounder
Diane de Poitiers	9/3/1499	Henry II (France)	Lover

You talk about yourself a great deal. That's why there are no distinctive characters in your writing. Your characters are all alike. You probably don't understand women; you've never depicted one successfully.

Leo Tolstoy, born 9/9/1828,
to Aries writer Maxim Gorki

I say sorry to my wife about five times a day for various reasons.

Harry Connick Jr.

Positive: Virgo with Libra

Libra charm penetrates Virgo reserve; Libra balance soothes Virgo anxiety. Virgo practicality helps the Libran idealist stay

grounded in reality. Virgo lies next to Libra on the zodiac circle. Adjacent astrological signs often enjoy solid relationships due to the high likelihood of overlapping zodiac signs for Mercury, planet of communication, and Venus, planet of affection. As seen from Earth, inner planets Mercury and Venus can be located no more than 28 and 48 degrees, respectively, from the individual's Sun. For any person with Sun in Virgo, Mercury must be in Leo, Virgo or Libra. Venus is apt to be located in Leo, Virgo or Libra.

Shared zodiac signs bring similar characteristics that enhance compatibility. Natal Mercury placed in Libra for Virgos Jada Pinkett Smith and Mike Comrie matches the Sun sign of their Libran spouses. The Libra Mercury and Virgo Sun of Sophia Loren blended well with Mercury in Virgo and Sun in Libra for her frequent costar Marcello Mastroianni.

Virgo	Birthdate	Libra	Relationship
Beyoncé	9/4/1981	Gwyneth Paltrow	Good friend
Mike Comrie	9/11/1980	Hilary Duff	Spouse
Michelle Williams	9/9/1980	Spike Jonze	Lover, split
Jada Pinkett Smith	9/18/1971	Will Smith	Spouse
Jack Black	8/28/1969	Tanya Haden	Spouse
Branford Marsalis	8/26/1960	Wynton Marsalis	Brother, music partner
Franco Amurri	9/12/1958	Susan Sarandon	Lover, parent
Mark Harmon	9/2/1951	Pam Dawber	Spouse
Frankie Avalon	9/18/1940	Annette Funicello	Beach movie costar
Alice Coltrane	8/27/1937	John Coltrane	Spouse, music collaborator
Sophia Loren	9/20/1934	Marcello Mastroianni	Costar, 15 movies
Antonia Fraser	8/27/1932	Harold Pinter	Spouse
Regis Philbin	8/25/1931	Kelly Ripa	Television cohost
Carol Matthau	9/11/1924	Walter Matthau	Spouse
Charlie Parker	8/29/1920	Dizzy Gillespie	Bebop partner
Isaac Funk	9/10/1839	Adam Wagnalls	Dictionary partner
Lucy Hayes	8/28/1831	Rutherford Hayes	Spouse

Respectful communication—we study with one another to see the core of the issue, uproot it, dissect it and handle it.
Jada Pinkett Smith about Will Smith

Communication is key—listening, sharing, finding a good TV show together. My wife and I have been really into Project Runway.
Jack Black about Tanya Haden

Positive: Virgo with Leo

Leo expects to be served; Virgo serves. Leo-Virgo makes a complementary pairing as Leo strides into the spotlight and Virgo contributes contentedly from behind the scenes. Virgo lies next to Leo in the zodiac circle. Adjacent astrological signs often enjoy solid relationships due to the high likelihood of overlapping zodiac signs for Mercury, planet of communication, and Venus, planet of affection. As seen from Earth, inner planets Mercury and Venus can be located no more than 28 and 48 degrees, respectively, from the individual's Sun. For any person with Sun in Virgo, Mercury must be in Leo, Virgo or Libra. Venus is apt to be located in Leo, Virgo or Libra.

Shared zodiac signs bring similar characteristics that enhance compatibility. Mercury in Virgo for Leo Madonna matches the Sun sign of her good friend, Virgo Jessica Seinfeld. Venus in Leo for Virgo Regis Philbin matches the Leo Sun of longtime cohost Kathie Lee Gifford. Leo presides over the big picture and Virgo tidies up the details.

Virgo	Birthdate	Leo	Relationship
Heidi Montag	9/15/1986	Spencer Pratt	Spouse
Emmy Rossum	9/12/1986	Adam Duritz	Lover, split
Macaulay Culkin	8/26/1980	Mila Kunis	Domestic partner, split
Nas	9/14/1973	Kelis	Spouse, divorced

Cameron Diaz	8/30/1972	Alex Rodriguez	Lover, split
Luke Wilson	9/21/1971	Pete Sampras	Best friend
Jessica Seinfeld	9/12/1971	Madonna	Close friend
Melissa McCarthy	8/26/1970	Billy Gardell	TV comedy costar
Marc Anthony	9/16/1968	Jennifer Lopez	Spouse, divorced
Guy Ritchie	9/10/1968	Madonna	Spouse, divorced
Rachael Ray	8/25/1968	John Cusimano	Spouse
Charlie Sheen	9/3/1965	Martin Sheen	Father; close
Keanu Reeves	9/2/1964	Sandra Bullock	Movie costar
Regis Philbin	8/25/1931	Kathie Lee Gifford	TV cohost
Lauren Bacall	9/16/1924	Jason Robards	Spouse, divorced
George Putnam	9/7/1887	Amelia Earhart	Spouse
D.H. Lawrence	9/11/1885	Frieda Lawrence	Spouse
Mary Shelley	8/30/1797	Percy Bysshe Shelley	Spouse

She's always in your face, isn't she? I don't get it. What is it about her? She's not a great dancer or singer. But she does know how to market herself. That must be it.

Michael Jackson, born 8/29/1958,
about Leo Madonna

She's always been the boss! That's the first thing a man has to know.

Marc Anthony about Jennifer Lopez

I've got a man who can cook, is a lawyer and a rock star. And he doesn't mind that I come home from work at 10 p.m. What idiot would divorce that?

Rachael Ray about John Cusimano

Positive: Virgo with Scorpio

Emotional Scorpio (Water) and practical Virgo (Earth) mix comfortably without either element dominating or disappearing. Scorpio's bold sexiness draws out the Virgin's latent sexuality.

Scorpio composure tempers Virgo anxiety, while Virgo analytical skills complement Scorpio's instinctive perception of the overall power structure.

Virgo	Birthdate	Scorpio	Relationship
Blake Lively	8/25/1987	Ryan Reynolds	Spouse
Blake Lively	8/25/1987	Penn Badgley	Boyfriend, split
Kimberly Williams-Paisley	9/14/1971	Brad Paisley	Spouse
Marc Anthony	9/16/1968	Dayanara Torres	Spouse, divorced
Shania Twain	8/28/1965	Robert Lange	Spouse, divorced
Domenico Dolce	9/13/1958	Stefano Gabbana	Fashion partner
Elvis Costello	8/25/1954	Diana Krall	Spouse
Richard Gere	8/31/1949	Julia Roberts	Movie costar
Bela Karolyi	9/13/1942	Nadia Comaneci	Gymnastics protégé
Warren Buffett	8/30/1930	Bill Gates	Business friend
Sarah Polk	9/4/1803	James Polk	Spouse
Goethe	8/28/1749	Friedrich Schiller	Literary friend
Samuel Johnson	9/18/1709	James Boswell	Friend, biography subject

[Scorpio] Robert De Niro's strength shines through, and that's very sexy.

Beyoncé, born 9/4/1981

If I'm not with someone
who really excites or inspires me,
then I'd rather be with myself.

Blake Lively, born 8/25/1987

Positive: Virgo with Cancer

Steady Virgo (Earth) and resilient Cancer (Water) blend easily without one element dominating the other. Virgo invests the daily effort that sustains Cancer's nurturing nest. Self-effacing Virgo lets Cancer the Crab be the boss.

Virgo	Birthdate	Cancer	Relationship
Prince Harry	9/15/1984	Prince William	Brother
Prince Harry	9/15/1984	Princess Diana	Mother
Chad Murray	8/24/1981	Sophia Bush	Spouse, divorced
Michelle Williams	9/9/1980	Busy Philipps	Best friend
Eric Johnson	9/15/1979	Jessica Simpson	Fiancée
Pink	9/8/1979	Carey Hart	Spouse
Michael Emerson	9/7/1954	Carrie Preston	Spouse
Jane Curtin	9/6/1947	Gilda Radner	Comedy partner
Barbara Bach	8/27/1947	Ringo Starr	Spouse
Anne Bancroft	9/17/1931	Mel Brooks	Spouse
Ferdinand Marcos	9/11/1917	Imelda Marcos	Spouse
Joseph Kennedy	9/6/1888	Rose Kennedy	Spouse
Queen Elizabeth I (Eng.)	9/17/1533	Robert Dudley	Rumored lover

I knew when I met him he'd be a great father, but watching him fall in love, watching him nurture her, I've never been so in love with him in my life. He keeps thanking me for giving her to him. It's a beautiful time.

Pink about Carey Hart

Very Positive: Virgo with Capricorn

Earth signs Virgo and Capricorn combine easily as energy flows smoothly around your 120-degree relationship on the zodiac circle. Virgo's grassroots thoroughness complements Capricorn's managerial focus on the big picture. Virgo and Capricorn share the capacity for self-discipline and the urge to be of service to others. Both Virgo and Capricorn function best in a stable environment.

Virgo	Birthdate	Capricorn	Relationship
Jason Derulo	9/21/1989	Jordin Sparks	Girlfriend
Evan Rachel Wood	9/7/1987	Marilyn Manson	Lover, split
Blake Lively	8/25/1987	Christian Louboutin	Close friend
Sean Foreman	8/27/1985	Nathaniel Motte	3OH!3 bandmate

Beyoncé	9/4/1981	Tina Knowles	Mother, design partner
Michelle Williams	9/9/1980	Jason Segel	Lover, split
Jason Sudeikis	9/18/1975	January Jones	Lover, split
Rose McGowan	9/5/1973	Marilyn Manson	Fiancé, split
Rachel Hunter	9/9/1969	Rod Stewart	Spouse, divorced
K-Ci	9/2/1969	Mary J. Blige	Lover, split
Robyn Gibson	9/15/1960	Mel Gibson	Spouse, divorced
Dave Stewart	9/9/1952	Annie Lennox	Eurythmics partner
Jerry Bruckheimer	9/21/1945	Nicolas Cage	Movie collaborator
Warren Buffett	8/30/1930	Charlie Munger	Investment partner
Richard Attenborough	8/29/1923	Anthony Hopkins	Longtime friend
Lyndon Johnson	8/27/1908	Lady Bird Johnson	Spouse

Charlie and I can handle a four-page memo over the phone with three grunts.
Warren Buffett about Charlie Munger

His sense of calm.
Rose McGowan, asked her favorite thing about Marilyn Manson

Very Positive: Virgo with Taurus

Projects flow well when shared by earth signs Taurus and Virgo. Virgo organizes the specifics before determined Taurus pushes the project through. Adaptable Virgo encourages Taurus to drop worn-out habits. Steady Taurus wears away the layers of Virgo reserve and lowers the volume on Virgo anxiety.

Virgo	Birthdate	Taurus	Relationship
Scott Moir	9/2/1987	Tessa Virtue	Olympic ice dance partner
Lea Michele	8/29/1986	Cory Monteith	Costar, lover
Paul McDonald	8/29/1984	Nikki Reed	Spouse
Elisabetta Canalis	9/12/1978	George Clooney	Lover, split
Michael Bublé	9/9/1975	Luisana Lopilato	Spouse

Jimmy Fallon	9/19/1974	Nancy Juvonen	Spouse
Amy Poehler	9/16/1971	Will Arnett	Spouse, divorced
Amy Poehler	9/16/1971	Tina Fey	SNL partner
Jessica Seinfeld	9/12/1971	Jerry Seinfeld	Spouse
Faith Hill	9/21/1967	Tim McGraw	Spouse
Salma Hayek	9/2/1966	Penelope Cruz	Best friend
Melissa Leo	9/14/1960	Barbra Streisand	Longtime friend
Candy Spelling	9/20/1945	Tori Spelling	Daughter
Candy Spelling	9/20/1945	Aaron Spelling	Spouse
Daryl Dragon	8/27/1942	Toni Tennille	Music partner, spouse
John McCain	8/29/1936	Cindy McCain	Spouse
Sophia Loren	9/20/1934	Audrey Hepburn	Longtime friend
George Jones	9/12/1931	Tammy Wynette	Spouse, divorced
Lauren Bacall	9/16/1924	Katharine Hepburn	50-year friend
Ingrid Bergman	8/29/1915	Roberto Rossellini	Spouse, divorced
David Packard	9/7/1912	William Hewlett	Business partner
Gala Dali	9/7/1894	Salvador Dali	Spouse
Agatha Christie	9/15/1890	Max Mallowan	Spouse

Tim has given me confidence and strength and my foundation. He makes me feel like I can conquer the world.

Faith Hill about Tim McGraw

We both have no problem looking like idiots to each other or other people. We will stand in the bathroom in front of our double sinks and have contests to see who can make the queerest, most disgusting face. It gets serious. Like, "Good job. How about this?"

Amy Poehler about Will Arnett

Very Positive: Virgo with Pisces

Opposites attract. Virgo and Pisces oppose each other on the zodiac circle and generally form complementary relationships. Virgo's analytical mind balances the Pisces preoccupation with the cosmos. Virgo suggests; Pisces tolerates. Virgo routines encourage Pisces discipline, while Pisces empathy softens the brisk tone of Virgo helpfulness.

Virgo	Birthdate	Pisces	Relationship
Evan Rachel Wood	9/7/1987	Jamie Bell	Spouse
Aaron Ross	9/15/1982	Sanya Richards	Spouse
Nicole Richie	9/21/1981	Joel Madden	Spouse
Jason Sudeikis	9/18/1975	Olivia Wilde	Fiancée
Michael Bublé	9/9/1975	Emily Blunt	Lover, split
Jennifer Nettles	9/12/1974	Kristian Bush	Music partner (Sugarland)
Cameron Diaz	8/30/1972	Drew Barrymore	Best friend
Camille Grammer	9/2/1968	Kelsey Grammer	Spouse, divorced
Adam Sandler	9/9/1966	Drew Barrymore	Movie costar
Charlie Sheen	9/3/1965	Bret Michaels	Good friend
Marlee Matlin	8/24/1965	William Hurt	Lover, split
Holly Robinson Peete	9/18/1964	Rodney Peete	Spouse
Melissa Leo	9/14/1960	John Heard	Lover, split
Michael Jackson	8/29/1958	Quincy Jones	Music collaborator
Michael Jackson	8/29/1958	Elizabeth Taylor	Good friend
Gloria Estefan	9/1/1957	Emilio Estefan	Spouse, manager
Richard Gere	8/31/1949	Cindy Crawford	Spouse, divorced
Peggy Lipton	8/30/1946	Quincy Jones	Spouse, divorced
Joan Kennedy	9/5/1935	Ted Kennedy	Spouse, divorced
Ray Charles	9/23/1930	Quincy Jones	Longtime friend
Sean Connery	8/25/1930	Michael Caine	Good friend
Christopher Isherwood	8/26/1904	W.H. Auden	Longtime friend

When I met Quincy, every other person fell away . . . This was the man I had been waiting for. A man who was open, affectionate, funny, smart and willing to truly give of himself.

Peggy Lipton about Quincy Jones

He's Pisces. We're polar; we balance each other. If we were both like him, we would have had a heart attack by now. If we were both like me, we would still be sitting back in the old house, watching TV.

Gloria Estefan about Emilio Estefan

We will figure out something, someday, absolutely. I have a good time with Drew.

Adam Sandler about doing more movies with Drew Barrymore

At Work

Looking for professional role models? Choose the leadership stability of England's Queen Elizabeth I (9/17/1533), the simple hands-on fiscal approach of billionaire Warren Buffett (8/30/1930) or the service orientation of political leader John McCain (8/29/1936).

- **Performance Anxiety**
- **Practical Solutions**
- **Money Smarts**
- **Consistent Effort**
- **Power Women**

Performance Anxiety

Virgo seeks perfection. Despite your hard work, you fret about doing an adequate job. Virgo celebrities admit getting anxious about meeting expectations.

> *I used to tremble from nerves so badly that the only way I could hold my head steady was to lower my chin practically to my chest and look up at Bogie. That was the beginning of The Look. I still get the shakes from time to time.*
>
> Lauren Bacall, born 9/16/1924

Success breeds complacency. Complacency breeds failure. Only the paranoid survive.

Andy Grove, born 9/2/1936

If I seem nervous, it's only because the show is a favorite of so many people. It's a classic. There's a lot of expectation. You know, they want me to come in here and just have a load of fun with Murphy. Really zap her.

Lily Tomlin, born 9/1/1937

Anybody who's really successful has doubts.

Jerry Bruckheimer, born 9/21/1945

I got away last year from what made me successful. I looked in the mirror and asked, "Is my talent dwindling?" Instead of thinking that you're going to have a long career, you're doubting yourself, worrying. This year I've gotten things more in focus, and it's taken away any doubts.

Cal Ripken Jr., born 8/24/1960

I panic with any job.

Hugh Grant, born 9/9/1960

I've never stuttered, but I've had the same drowning feeling from stage fright. When I forget my lines, I forget who I am, where I am. It feels like an eternity until I come back.

Colin Firth, born 9/10/1960

It's always the first working day for me, getting accustomed to the crew.

Kevin Zegers, born 9/19/1984,
asked about his toughest scene

I had never acted before. I was nervous, but I got used to it.

9-year-old Oscar nominee Quvenzhané Wallis, born 8/28/2003, about acting in Beasts of the Southern Wild

Practical Solutions

Virgo wants to make practical contributions to the team. Your analytical mind dissects the immediate problem for answers. Virgo is one of the zodiac's most adept signs at puzzling through to workable solutions.

If I didn't start painting, I would have raised chickens.

Grandma Moses, born 9/7/1860

There will always be a place for anyone with a good and practical idea, willing to work unstintingly to get it accepted and translated into terms of the service of practical use.

J.C. Penney, born 9/16/1875

Problems are the price of progress. Don't bring me anything but trouble.

Charles Kettering, born 8/29/1876

A problem well stated is a problem half solved.

Charles Kettering, born 8/29/1876

I can improvise things when in difficulties—this has been a most useful accomplishment; the things I can do with hairpins and safety pins when in domestic difficulties would surprise you. It was I who fashioned bread into a sticky pill, stuck it on a hairpin, attached the hairpin with sealing wax on the end of a window pole, and managed to pick up my mother's false teeth from where they had fallen on to the conservatory roof! I successfully

chloroformed a hedgehog that was entangled in the tennis net and so managed to release it. I can claim to be useful about the house.

Agatha Christie, born 9/15/1890

All difficult problems have easy, simple,
understandable, wrong solutions.

Laurence Peter, born 9/16/1919

Someone's sitting in the shade today because
someone planted a tree a long time ago.

Warren Buffett, born 8/30/1930

Not all problems have a technological answer, but
when they do, that is the more lasting solution.

Andy Grove, born 9/2/1936

I think of myself as a problem-solver. I want to go
in and help the director and the writer to get the
best they can out of the text they're working with.

Michael Emerson, born 9/7/1954

When I receive letters from people telling me
that I've helped them in some way to overcome
the fear of the kitchen, then I know I've done
my job and I've made a difference.

Rachael Ray, born 8/25/1968

I'm always tinkering with something—suddenly
I'll think I can work with wood, but then I'll
realize I can't, so I go back to sewing.

Melissa McCarthy, born 8/26/1970

Money Smarts

Virgo contributes financial evaluation. Your ease with numerical analysis keeps you in touch with the dollars and cents. Unpretentious investor Warren Buffett (8/30/1930) is the early 21st-century icon for plainspoken financial wisdom.

Rule No. 1: Never lose money.
Rule No. 2: Never forget Rule No. 1.
Warren Buffett, born 8/30/1930

Investment must be rational; if you can't understand it, don't do it.
Warren Buffett, born 8/30/1930

The counting-house of an accomplished merchant is a school of method wherein the great science may be learned of ranging particulars under generals, of bringing the different parts of a transaction together, and of showing at one view a long series of dealing and exchange.
Samuel Johnson, born 9/18/1709

What advantages a merchant derives from double entry bookkeeping! It is among the finest inventions of the human mind; and every good householder should introduce it into his economy.
Goethe, born 8/28/1749
Wilhelm Meister's Apprenticeship

To get what I want, I pay as much as I have to and as little as I can get away with.
Samuel Goldwyn, born 8/27/1882

That I liked arithmetic seemed strange to my mother, who had never, as she admitted freely, had any use for figures, and had so much trouble with household accounts that my father took them over.

Agatha Christie, born 9/15/1890

Employ every economy consistent with thoroughness, accuracy and reliability.

Arthur Nielsen, born 9/5/1897

Immediately, I saw that we were a rock 'n roll brand, not just a rock 'n roll band. See, the rest of the guys with guitars around their necks want credibility. I don't want credibility. That means nothing.

Gene Simmons, born 8/25/1949

[My father] would get his $800 a week and be ecstatic, and then I'd watch the man who owned the house sell it and make $80,000 in profit. So what I learned early on was, "Be the man who owns the house."

Tyler Perry, born 9/13/1969

Consistent Effort

Earth signs Taurus, Capricorn and Virgo bring a steady presence to any workplace. Capricorn makes the master manager while Taurus the Bull provides the stubborn strength that overcomes obstacles. Diligent plugging away at the daily chores makes Virgo the worker bee of the zodiac.

'Tis ambition enough to be employed as an under-laborer in clearing ground a little, and removing some of the rubbish that lies in the way of knowledge.

John Locke, born 8/29/1632

Without haste, but without rest.
Motto of Goethe, born 8/28/1749

In the realm of ideas all depends on enthusiasm;
in the real world all rests on perseverance.
Goethe, born 8/28/1749

Keep on going and the chances are that you will
stumble on something, perhaps when you are
least expecting it. I have never heard of anyone
stumbling on something sitting down.
Charles Kettering, born 8/29/1876

Success seems to be largely a matter of
hanging on after others have let go.
William Feather, born 8/25/1889

Never give up. Never. Show them
that ugly can be beautiful.
Agnes de Mille, born 9/18/1905

When the press talks about my successes as Senate majority leader they always emphasize my capacity to persuade, to wheel and deal. Hardly anyone ever mentions that I usually had more and better information than my colleagues.
Lyndon Johnson, born 8/27/1908

Just keep going. Everybody gets better if they keep at it.
Ted Williams, born 8/30/1918

I think I was born strong-willed. That's not the
kind of thing you can learn. The advantage
is, you stick to what you believe in and rarely
get pushed out of what you want to do.
Joan Jett, born 9/22/1960

Power Women

There's nothing like a little girl power—with muscle.
Jada Pinkett Smith, born 9/18/1971

Thousands of years ago, the virgin goddess symbolized magical, life-giving strength. Harvest goddesses Isis and Demeter provided the essential annual crops. Each Vestal Virgin contributed 30 years to guard the ritual hearth fires of Rome. The Biblical Virgin Mary still provides sustenance for millions around the world. More than any other zodiac sign, Virgo contributes a succession of strong, pioneering lady leaders. Virgo power women survive independent and unscathed in male-dominated environments.

Lady Virgo Leader	Birthdate	Known as:
Diane de Poitiers	9/3/1499	Influential mistress of French king
Elizabeth I	9/17/1533	44-year Queen of England
Dixy Lee Ray	9/3/1914	Outspoken Washington Governor
Ann Richards	9/1/1933	Proactive Texas Governor
Geraldine Ferraro	8/26/1935	First lady major-party VP candidate
Drew Gilpin Faust	9/18/1947	Harvard's first female President
Queen Rania (Jordan)	8/31/1970	Visible Arab role model

I have the heart of a man, not a woman,
and I am not afraid of anything.
Queen Elizabeth I, born 9/17/1533

I was cordial, tried to appear relaxed . . . [David] kept calling the women over to dance on top of the table. The other men were either slightly amused or embarrassed . . . The next day in the office the balance of power had shifted perceptibly. I had shown . . . that I would not be intimidated.
Carly Fiorina, born 9/6/1954

Virgo Politicians

In addition to the lady leaders already listed, Virgo contributes the following political figures.

Virgo Politician	Birthdate	Position:
Chris Christie	9/6/1962	New Jersey Governor
Scott Brown	9/12/1959	Massachusetts Senator
Mike Huckabee	8/24/1955	Arkansas Governor
John McCain	8/29/1936	Arizona Senator, Presidential candidate
Yasser Arafat	8/24/1929	Palestinian Liberation chair
Paul Volcker	9/5/1927	U.S. economic advisor
George Wallace	8/15/1919	16-year Alabama Governor
Ferdinand Marcos	9/11/1917	Philippine dictator
Kwame Nkrumah	9/21/1909	Ghana leader; Pan-Africanism advocate
Lyndon Johnson	8/27/1908	U.S. President, War on Poverty
Walter Reuther	9/1/1907	Union leader (UAW)
Huey Long	8/30/1893	Louisiana political dynasty patriarch
Joseph Kennedy	9/6/1888	U.S. political dynasty patriarch
William Taft	9/15/1857	Task-oriented U.S. President
Porfirio Diaz	9/15/1830	Mexican President
Marquis de Lafayette	9/6/1757	American Revolution general
Louis XIV	9/5/1638	72-year French "Sun King"
Cardinal Richelieu	9/9/1585	Chief Minister of Louis XIII (France)
Richard the Lionheart	9/15/1157	King of England, Crusade leader
Caligula	8/31/12	Tyrannical Roman Emperor

I don't know what will be written about my administration . . . But I would hope that it would be said of this decade, if not of this administration, so far as the ancient enemies of mankind are concerned . . . [we coped with] those ancient enemies . . . ignorance, illiteracy, ill health, and disease.

Lyndon Johnson, born 8/27/1908

Nothing is more liberating than to fight for a cause larger than yourself, something that encompasses you but is not defined by your existence alone.

John McCain, born 8/29/1936
Faith of My Fathers

I don't compromise my principles for politics.

Chris Christie, born 9/6/1962

Virgo Business Leaders

Virgo Leader	Birthdate	Known for:
Tyler Perry	9/13/1969	Highest paid man in entertainment
Debbi Fields	9/18/1956	Mrs. Fields Cookies
Carly Fiorina	9/6/1954	Hewlett-Packard CEO
Karen Mills	9/14/1953	SBA administrator
Colleen Barrett	9/14/1944	Southwest Airlines President
Peter Ueberroth	9/2/1937	Sports executive
Andy Grove	9/2/1936	Intel CEO
Brian Epstein	9/19/1934	Beatles business manager
Warren Buffett	8/30/1930	Lucrative investments
Sydney Harris	9/14/1917	Consumer polls
John Marriott	9/17/1900	Hotel chain
Arthur Nielsen	9/5/1897	Television ratings system
Alfred Knopf	9/12/1892	Book publishing
Colonel Sanders	9/9/1890	Fried chicken
J.C. Penney	9/16/1875	Department store
Edward Filene	9/3/1860	Department store
Milton Hershey	9/13/1857	Chocolate
David Buick	9/17/1855	Cars
Albert Spalding	9/2/1850	Sporting goods company
George Cadbury	9/19/1839	Candy
Allan Pinkerton	8/25/1819	Detective agency

Watch every detail that affects the accuracy of your work.

Arthur Nielsen, born 9/5/1897

When it comes to getting things done, we need fewer architects and more bricklayers.

Colleen Barrett, born 9/14/1944

Virgo Scientists

Virgo Scientist	Birthdate	Discovery / Invention
Chen Ning Yang	9/22/1922	Physicist
Marvin Middlemark	9/16/1919	Rabbit Ears (TV reception)
Albert Sabin	8/26/1906	Polio vaccine
Charles Kettering	8/29/1876	Electrical starter, leaded gasoline
Walter Reed	9/13/1851	Yellow fever caused by mosquitoes
Michael Faraday	9/22/1791	Electromagnetism
Antoine Lavoisier	8/26/1743	Father of modern chemistry

Whenever you look at a piece of work and you think the fellow was crazy, then you want to pay some attention to that. One of you is likely to be, and you had better find out which one it is. It makes an awful lot of difference.

Charles Kettering, born 8/29/1876

Creativity

Virgo art—the deceptively simple moves of Michael Jackson, Tolstoy's precise depictions of war and domesticity, the classy self-projection of entertainers Sophia Loren and Beyoncé.

- **Technical Proficiency**
- **Intellect and Wit**
- **Odd Humor**
- **Skill with the Grotesque**

Technical Proficiency

Virgo artists invest time and effort on technique. Jacques-Louis David (8/30/1748) and Jean Ingres (8/29/1780) led art's Neoclassical return to detail and perspective. Saxophonist Charlie Parker (8/29/1920) and Itzhak Perlman (8/31/1945) are recognized as virtuoso musicians. Virgo entertainers like Michael Jackson (8/29/1958) and Beyoncé (9/4/1981) orchestrate every detail of their stage shows.

I feel like now I can be picky in what I do. I can take time to do it right.

Beyoncé, born 9/4/1981

The smallest hair throws its shadow.

Goethe, born 8/28/1749

You have to observe flowers in order to find
the right tones for the folds of clothes.

Jean Ingres, born 8/29/1780

I paint from the top down. First the sky, then
the mountains, then the hills, then the houses,
then the cattle, and then the people.

Grandma Moses, born 9/7/1860

She worked hard and studied hard and concentrated
on her job. That's why she was a star. She not only
had talent but she polished the talent, made it shine.

about Claudette Colbert, born 9/13/1903
Remark from Sagittarian Douglas Fairbanks Jr.

It takes great passion and great energy to do anything creative, especially in the theater. You have to care so much that you can't sleep, you can't eat, you can't talk to people. It's just got to be right. You can't do it without that passion.

Agnes de Mille, born 9/18/1905

I took corrective exercises to straighten up and stand tall. I learned intonations, how to breathe . . . voice inflections . . . how not to press that word, that word is unimportant, throw it away. I never stopped learning.

Ingrid Bergman, born 8/29/1915

Technique is communication: the two
words are synonymous in conductors.

Leonard Bernstein, born 8/25/1918

You've got to learn your instrument. Then, you practice, practice, practice. And then, when you finally get up there on the bandstand, forget all that and just wail.

Charlie Parker, born 8/29/1920

I'm never pleased with anything, I'm a perfectionist, it's part of who I am.

Michael Jackson, born 8/29/1958

I'm a perfectionist, so I always feel there's room for improvement.

Ludacris, born 9/11/1977

Virgo Specialty: Quirky Entertainers

Virgo masters some unique skills through experimentation and practice. Virgo delivers the zodiac's most extensive list of one-of-a-kind entertainers, often able to sustain popularity for extended periods of time.

Virgo Entertainer	Birthdate	Known for:
Honey Boo Boo	8/28/2005	Reality television star
Pink	9/8/1979	Gymnastic feats during concerts
Cesar Millan	8/27/1969	The Dog Whisperer
Kevin Clash	9/17/1960	18-year Elmo puppeteer
David Copperfield	9/16/1956	Magician
Shari Belafonte	9/22/1954	Puppeteer
Paul Reubens	8/27/1952	Children's TV host
Anna Deavere Smith	9/18/1950	One-person stage shows
Lola Falana	9/11/1942	Queen of Las Vegas
Robin Leach	8/29/1941	Lifestyles of the Rich and Famous
Allen Funt	9/16/1914	Candid Camera

I don't think necessity is the mother of invention. Invention, in my opinion, arises directly from idleness, possibly laziness, to save myself trouble.

Agatha Christie, born 9/15/1890

Mama says pretty comes in all sizes, and mine is cute.

Honey Boo Boo, born 8/28/2005

Intellect and Wit

Intellectual intricacy drives Virgo art. You observe, you dissect, you assess, you test, you speak. Innovative verbal content characterizes the songs written by contemporary musicians Van Morrison (8/31/1945), Elvis Costello (8/25/1954) and Jack Black (8/28/1969). Virgo fills the creative product with subtle witticisms.

The chief consideration for a good painter is to think out the whole of his picture, to have it in his head as a whole . . . so that he may then execute it with warmth and as if the entire thing were done at the same time.

Jean Ingres, born 8/29/1780

I'm a natural piano player. So all the practicing I do at this point is in my head. If I don't play for a year, my chops aren't going to get any worse. I've spent my time playing scales, and I don't necessarily want to play any faster than I play. So everything I do at this point is more philosophical.

Harry Connick Jr., born 9/11/1967

Virgo Specialty: Leading Rappers

Ever-verbal Virgo tops the list of famous rappers along with Gemini and Libra.

Rap / Hip-Hop	Birthdate	Known for:
Wiz Khalifa	9/8/1987	Black and Yellow
Wale	9/21/1984	Lotus Flower Bomb
Ludacris	9/11/1977	Money Maker
Bizzy Bone	9/12/1976	Rapid fire Chopper style
Nas	9/14/1973	Illmatic
Big Daddy Kane	9/10/1968	Fast rhyming
Eazy-E	9/7/1963	Godfather of Gangsta Rap

I came up with my first official song when I was 9. It was funny, because I came up with a line then that went, "I'm cool / I'm bad / I might be 9 / But I can't survive without my girlfriend." So I changed my age, in the song at least, to 10. Even then, I knew it had to rhyme.

Ludacris, born 9/11/1977

Odd Humor

Virgo's strange sense of humor gladly uses physical contortion and crazed silliness to get a laugh. Virgo contributes Peter Sellers (9/8/1925) as the clumsy inspector in the old Pink Panther movies and the comedic goofballs Lily Tomlin (9/1/1937), Bill Murray (9/21/1950), Adam Sandler (9/9/1966) and Amy Poehler (9/16/1971).

He who lives without folly is not as wise as he thinks.

François de La Rochefoucauld, born 9/15/1613

By nothing do men show their character
more than by the things they laugh at.

Goethe, born 8/28/1749

The memory of my confident anticipations of a profoundly grave and intellectual posterity came, with irresistible merriment, to my mind.

H.G. Wells, born 9/21/1866
The Time Machine

You can't deny laughter; when it comes, it plops down in your favorite chair and stays as long as it wants.

Stephen King, born 9/21/1947

I've played villains on stage—you know, the Iagos and so on—but I think of myself as a funny person. I mostly did comedies before I did TV work.

Michael Emerson, born 9/7/1954

My comedy is different every time I do it. I don't know what the hell I'm doing.

Adam Sandler, born 9/9/1966

You can't go halfway. If you don't allow yourself to look crazy and silly, your vanity will get in the way.

Amy Poehler, born 9/16/1971

Virgo Specialty: #1 in Cartoonists

Talents for humor, detail and repetition combine to make Virgo the zodiac sign with the most famous cartoonists. Comic strips conveniently allow veiled judgment and criticism.

Virgo Cartoonist	Birthdate	Known for:
Cathy Guisewite	9/5/1950	Cathy
Jeff MacNelly	9/17/1947	Shoe; editorial cartoons
Robert Crumb	8/30/1943	Felix the Cat
Mort Walker	9/3/1923	Beetle Bailey
Alex Anderson	9/5/1920	Rocky and Bullwinkle
Brant Parker	8/26/1920	The Wizard of Id

Jack Kirby	8/28/1917	Captain America
Walt Kelly	8/25/1913	Pogo
Ted Key	8/25/1912	Hazel
Gus Edson	9/20/1901	The Gumps
Jimmy Hatlo	9/1/1897	They'll Do It Every Time
Frank Willard	9/21/1893	Moon Mullins
John Striebel	9/14/1891	Dixie Dugan
Kin Hubbard	9/1/1868	Abe Martin of Brown County

The most perfect caricature is that which, on a small surface, with the simplest means, most accurately exaggerates, to the highest point, the peculiarities of a human being, at his most characteristic moment in the most beautiful manner.

Max Beerbohm, born 8/24/1872

There is no voice for that state of being grown-up, and being surrounded by every human being who is part of a couple or family. I won't abandon her.

Cathy Guisewite, born 9/5/1950, asked if she'd marry off her single, neurotic character when she herself wed

Skill with the Grotesque

The extreme, tense Virgo imagination explores situations without human sensitivity and decorum. Mary Shelley (8/30/1797) created the long-lived monster Frankenstein. *Lord of the Flies* from William Golding (9/19/1911) shows the ugly proclivities of boys left to nature. Stephen King (9/21/1947) is today's premier writer of horror fiction.

You can't write well with only the nice parts of your character, and only about nice things. And I don't want even to try anymore. I want to use everything, including hate and envy and lust and fear.

Alison Lurie, born 9/3/1926

The great artists of the world are never Puritans, and seldom even ordinarily respectable.

H.L. Mencken, born 9/12/1880

While an undergraduate at Oxford, I used to go to read in the British Museum reading room. Looking up from my book, I was often fascinated by the eccentric-looking elderly ladies at neighboring desks. After letting my imagination play on them for some time, I wrote a piece for the college magazine called "Witches at the Museum." Shortly after it appeared, I was sent for by the principal. It seemed that the people I had described, far from having, as I supposed, emerged from obscure bed-sitters, were eminent scholars from other universities. I had described them so vividly that she recognized them all. Since I had depicted them engaged in sorcery, vampirism of infants, and similar pursuits, and was informed that some of them took the magazine, this interview comes fairly high in my embarrassment scale.

Mary Renault, born 9/4/1905

I saw the pale student of unhallowed arts kneeling beside the thing he had put together. I saw the hideous phantasm of a man stretched out, and then, on the working of some powerful engine, show signs of life, and stir with an uneasy, half vital motion. Frightful must it be; for supremely frightful would be the effect of any human endeavor to mock the stupendous mechanism of the Creator of the world.

Mary Shelley, born 8/30/1797,
about the birth of Frankenstein

Kill the beast! Cut his throat! Spill his blood!

William Golding, born 9/19/1911
Lord of the Flies, refrain among the boys

I shoot good violence. I mean, I know I do.

Oliver Stone, born 9/15/1946

When he comes out and he vomits . . . and he sees these nurse's legs sticking out and there are these worms crawling all over them . . . it's sort of a special moment for me.

Stephen King, born 9/21/1947,
describing a favorite scene

People want to know why I do this, why I write such gross stuff. I like to tell them I have the heart of a small boy—and I keep it in a jar on my desk.

Stephen King, born 9/21/1947

Virgo Writers

This list includes recent popular novelists and classic writers typically covered in collegiate literature studies. Pragmatic Virgo contributes fewer poets than other zodiac signs.

Virgo Writer	Birthdate	Known for:
Alice Sebold	9/6/1963	The Lovely Bones
Stephen King	9/21/1947	Horror and suspense novels
Antonia Fraser	8/27/1932	Historical fiction
Fay Weldon	9/22/1931	Feminist novels
Mary Stewart	9/17/1916	Series of novels about Merlin
Roald Dahl	9/13/1916	Charlie and the Chocolate Factory
William Golding	9/19/1911	Lord of the Flies
Richard Wright	9/4/1908	Native Son
Mary Renault	9/4/1905	Novels about Ancient Greece
James Hilton	9/9/1900	Lost Horizon; Goodbye, Mr. Chips

Taylor Caldwell	9/7/1900	Popular historical fiction
C.S. Forester	8/27/1899	Horatio Hornblower series
Jorge Luis Borges	8/24/1899	Magical realism
Agatha Christie	9/15/1890	Hercule Poirot, Miss Marple
Edith Sitwell	9/7/1887	Poetry collections
D.H. Lawrence	9/11/1885	Sons and Lovers
Elinor Wylie	9/7/1885	Sensuous poetry
Guillaume Apollinaire	8/26/1880	Calligrammes
Upton Sinclair	9/20/1878	The Jungle
Sherwood Anderson	9/13/1876	Winesburg, Ohio
Theodore Dreiser	8/27/1871	Sister Carrie
Edgar Lee Masters	8/23/1868	Spoon River Anthology
H.G. Wells	9/21/1866	The Invisible Man
O. Henry	9/11/1862	Short stories
Eugene Field	9/2/1850	Wynken, Blynken, and Nod
Sarah Orne Jewett	9/3/1849	Stories about the Maine coast
Charles Sanders Peirce	9/10/1839	Father of pragmatism
Bret Harte	8/25/1836	Stories about California pioneers
Leo Tolstoy	9/9/1828	Anna Karenina, War and Peace
Mary Shelley	8/30/1797	Frankenstein
James Fenimore Cooper	9/15/1789	The Last of the Mohicans
Georg Hegel	8/27/1770	Idealistic philosophy
Goethe	8/28/1749	Faust
Samuel Johnson	9/18/1709	Essays, poems, dictionary

If any wish to write in a clear style, let him be first clear in his thoughts; and if any would write in a noble style, let him first possess a noble soul.

Goethe

Write anything. Bad sentences, meaningless sentences, anything to get the mind fixed again to that sheet of paper and oblivious of the "real" world. Write until the words begin to make sense,

the cogs mesh, the wheels start to turn, the creaking movement quickens and becomes a smooth, oiled run, and then, with luck, exhaustion will be forgotten, and the real writing will begin.

Mary Stewart
The Stormy Petrel

Virgo Visual Artists

The detailed images of Virgos Grandma Moses and Jean Ingres contrast with Picasso's Scorpionic sexuality and Van Gogh's Arien haste. Well-known contributors to Western art history include the following Virgos:

Virgo Painter	Birthdate	Known for:
Morris Graves	8/28/1910	Expressionism, mysticism
Graham Sutherland	8/24/1903	Surrealistic landscapes
Grandma Moses	9/7/1860	Primitive landscapes
Edward Burne-Jones	8/28/1833	The Beguiling of Merlin
Jean Ingres	8/29/1780	Neoclassicism; portraits
Caspar Friedrich	9/5/1774	Allegorical landscapes
Jacques-Louis David	8/30/1748	Detailed classical scenes
George Stubbs	9/4/1724	Horse paintings

To give a body and a perfect form to one's thought,
this—and only this—is to be an artist.

Jacques-Louis David

Virgo Designer	Birthdate	Known for:
Nicole Richie	9/21/1981	House of Harlow accessories
Nate Berkus	9/17/1971	Home design expert
Stella McCartney	9/13/1971	Collaborations
Rachel Zoe	9/1/1971	Fashions for slim women
Domenico Dolce	9/13/1958	Luxury clothes and accessories
Karl Lagerfeld	9/10/1933	Head Chanel designer
Elsa Schiaparelli	9/10/1890	Playful, "anything goes"

I don't think that people should wear dresses two sizes too small. I just think that sexiness is better left to the imagination. It's just more tasteful.

Rachel Zoe

Virgo Illustrator	Birthdate	Known for:
Charles Gibson	9/14/1867	The Gibson Girl

I'll tell you how I got what you have called the "Gibson Girl." I saw her on the streets, I saw her at the theatres, I saw her in the churches. I saw her everywhere and doing everything. I saw her idling on Fifth Avenue and at work behind the counters of the stores.

Charles Gibson

Virgo Composers

Virgo Composer	Birthdate	Known for:
Paul Williams	9/19/1940	We've Only Just Begun
Maurice Jarre	9/13/1924	Movie scores
Leonard Bernstein	8/25/1918	West Side Story
John Cage	9/5/1912	4'33"
Arnold Schoenberg	9/13/1874	Expressionism, atonality
Antonin Dvorak	9/8/1841	New World Symphony
Anton Bruckner	9/4/1824	Romantic symphonies
Giacomo Meyerbeer	9/5/1791	Opera

For Ryan's Daughter I used a total of eight harps, something that was, at least, weird.

Maurice Jarre

Virgo Grammys for Record / Album of the Year

The most prestigious Grammys are awarded for Album, Record and Song of the Year. Song of the Year goes to the composer, often unknown except within the music industry. This Grammy list includes only those Virgos awarded with Album or Record of the Year. Virgo members of winning music groups are listed when holding a prominent position in the group. Go to www.QuotableZodiac.com for astrological updates on all annual awards.

Virgo Musician	Birthdate	Record / Album
Amy Winehouse	9/14/1983	Rehab
Charles Kelley (Lady Antebellum)	9/11/1981	Need You Now
Michael Jackson	8/29/1958	Beat It
Michael Jackson	8/29/1958	Thriller
Barry Gibb (Bee Gees)	9/1/1947	Saturday Night Fever
Daryl Dragon (with Tennille)	8/27/1942	Love Will Keep Us Together
David Clayton-Thomas	9/13/1941	Blood, Sweat & Tears
Ray Charles (with Norah Jones)	9/23/1930	Here We Go Again
Ray Charles	9/23/1930	Genius Loves Company
Bob Newhart	9/5/1929	Button Down Mind

I'm my own worst critic, and if I don't
pull off what I think I wanted to do in my
head, then I won't be a happy girl.

Amy Winehouse

Contemporary Virgo Musicians

Virgo Pop / Rock	Birthdate	Known for:
Niall Horan	9/13/1993	One Direction
Liam Payne	8/29/1993	One Direction
Nick Jonas	9/16/1992	Jonas Brothers
Jason Derulo	9/21/1989	In My Head

Florence Welch	8/28/1986	Florence + the Machine
Sean Foreman	8/27/1985	3OH!3
Beyoncé	9/4/1981	Popular hits and performances
Pink	9/8/1979	Missundaztood
Jack Black	8/28/1969	Satirical rock
Marc Anthony	9/16/1968	Amar Sin Mentiras
Moby	9/11/1965	Electronic dance music
Elvis Costello	8/25/1954	Diverse genres
Chrissie Hynde	9/7/1951	The Pretenders
Gene Simmons	8/25/1949	KISS
Freddie Mercury	9/5/1946	Queen
Van Morrison	8/31/1945	Moondance
Barry White	9/12/1944	Disco hits
Cass Elliot	9/19/1941	The Mamas & the Papas
Buddy Holly	9/7/1936	That'll Be the Day

I'm pretty confident and, at the same time, I'm pretty insecure. I'm like a walking conflict.

Pink

It just seems like musicians want to sell a few records and put out a perfume line, and I think it's so sad that there are so many musicians who don't want to change the world.

Moby

Virgo Specialty: Country Singers

Virgo contributes the pioneering men of country music. Starting with Patsy Cline, Virgo claims more lady country singers than any other zodiac sign. In the late 90s, Virgo often claimed the majority of the female nominees for annual singing awards—typically Faith Hill, Jo Dee Messina, LeAnn Rimes, Shania Twain, and / or Trisha Yearwood. Virgo's down-to-earth presentation and restrained

sexuality matched the expectations of country music fans. Today's country scene has evolved to the more overt sexuality of Scorpio Miranda Lambert.

> *Even on the sex symbol side of things, I'm very careful not to be sexual. And I think (this approach) rubs off in a healthy way for young women. I wish I had someone when I was 13 say, "You can wear things that are flattering. You don't have to be afraid your body is changing. But do it on a comfortable level."*
>
> Shania Twain

Virgo Country	Birthdate	Known for:
Hunter Hayes	9/9/1991	Wanted
LeAnn Rimes	8/28/1982	Blue
Jennifer Nettles	9/12/1974	Sugarland
Jo Dee Messina	8/25/1970	I'm Alright
Faith Hill	9/21/1967	Breathe
Shania Twain	8/28/1965	Come On Over (#1 album by woman)
Trisha Yearwood	9/19/1964	How Do I Live
Conway Twitty	9/1/1933	55 #1 hits
Patsy Cline	9/8/1932	Crazy
George Jones	9/12/1931	She Thinks I Still Care
Hank Williams	9/17/1923	I'm So Lonesome I Could Cry
Roy Acuff	9/15/1903	"King of Country Music"
Jimmie Rodgers	9/8/1897	"Father of Country Music"

> *You got to have smelt a lot of mule manure*
> *before you can sing like a hillbilly.*
>
> Hank Williams

Classical / Jazz / Blues	Birthdate	Known for:
Harry Connick Jr.	9/11/1967	Only You
Branford Marsalis	8/26/1960	Jazz quartet
Andrea Bocelli	9/22/1958	Sacred Arias

Itzhak Perlman	8/31/1945	Violin performance
Ray Charles	9/23/1930	What'd I Say
B.B. King	9/16/1925	Blues guitar (Lucille)
Dinah Washington	8/29/1924	"Queen of the Blues"
Charlie Parker	8/29/1920	Virtuoso sax

Don't play the saxophone. Let it play you.
Charlie Parker, born 8/29/1920

Virgo Academy Awards

Oscars for outstanding film achievement have been awarded each year since 1928. The following actor and actress lists include Virgo winners in both lead and supporting roles.

Oscar-Winning Actress	Birthdate	Movie
Jennifer Hudson	9/12/1981	Dreamgirls
Marlee Matlin	8/24/1965	Children of a Lesser God
Melissa Leo	9/14/1960	The Fighter
Sophia Loren	9/20/1934	Two Women
Anne Bancroft	9/17/1931	The Miracle Worker
Ingrid Bergman	8/29/1915	Murder on the Orient Express
Ingrid Bergman	8/29/1915	Anastasia
Ingrid Bergman	8/29/1915	Gaslight
Greta Garbo	9/18/1905	Honorary Academy award
Claudette Colbert	9/13/1903	It Happened One Night
Shirley Booth	8/30/1898	Come Back, Little Sheba

I made my living from looking young. I looked unspoilt.
It was really a good thing that I stopped in time.
There are a lot of people who go on far too long.
Greta Garbo

My body has done for me all these years things I couldn't ever even dreamt to do for characters. It's a tool, molecularly speaking, and I need to take care of it.

Melissa Leo

Oscar-Winning Actor	Birthdate	Movie
Colin Firth	9/10/1960	The King's Speech
Ed Begley Jr.	9/16/1949	Sweet Bird of Youth
Jeremy Irons	9/19/1948	Reversal of Fortune
Tommy Lee Jones	9/15/1946	The Fugitive
George Chakiris	9/16/1934	West Side Story
Sean Connery	8/25/1930	The Untouchables
James Coburn	8/31/1928	Affliction
Cliff Robertson	9/9/1925	Charly
Edmond O'Brien	9/10/1915	The Barefoot Contessa
John Houseman	9/22/1902	The Paper Chase
Fredric March	8/31/1897	The Best Years of Our Lives
Fredric March	8/31/1897	Dr. Jekyll and Mr. Hyde
Paul Muni	9/22/1895	Story of Louis Pasteur

I'd like to thank security for letting me into the building.

Colin Firth, accepting SAG award

Characters who live on the outer edge of acceptable behavior have always been to my taste.

Jeremy Irons

Oscar-Winning Director	Birthdate	Movie
Ethan Coen (with Sagittarian brother Joel)	9/21/1957	No Country for Old Men
Oliver Stone	9/15/1946	Born on the Fourth of July
Oliver Stone	9/15/1946	Platoon
William Friedkin	8/29/1939	The French Connection

Richard Attenborough	8/29/1923	Gandhi
Robert Wise	9/10/1914	The Sound of Music
Robert Wise	9/10/1914	West Side Story
Elia Kazan	9/7/1909	On the Waterfront
Elia Kazan	9/7/1909	Gentleman's Agreement

I really think that sex always looks kind of funny in a movie.

William Friedkin

Virgo Emmys

The annual Emmy Awards recognize excellence on television. With lead and supporting honors in drama, comedy, miniseries and guest appearances, almost 1,000 acting Emmys have been awarded since 1949. Outstanding performances often receive consecutive awards as a television series continues its run. So the following lists include only multiple winners—Virgos who won at least two Emmy awards either on different programs or with repeated honors for the same role.

Emmy-Winning Actor	Birthdate	Show(s)
Aaron Paul	8/27/1979	Breaking Bad
Eric Stonestreet	9/9/1971	Modern Family
James Gandolfini	9/18/1961	The Sopranos
Michael Emerson	9/7/1954	The Practice, LOST
Peter Falk	9/16/1927	Columbo
Sid Caesar	9/8/1922	Variety programs

The most important thing for me as an actor playing a character is to make you laugh. That's my No. 1 goal.

Eric Stonestreet

I love playing odd roles.

Aaron Paul

Emmy-Winning Actress	Birthdate	Show
Kristen Johnston	9/20/1967	3rd Rock from the Sun
Kristy McNichol	9/9/1962	Family
Jane Curtin	9/6/1947	Kate & Allie
Barbara Bain	9/13/1931	Mission: Impossible
Ingrid Bergman	8/29/1915	Specials
Shirley Booth	8/30/1898	Hazel

I love that Bill Gardell is just a cop and I'm just a teacher and we don't have secret lives where we're wrestling Russian alligators.

Melissa McCarthy, born 8/26/1970,
about Mike & Molly

Hollywood's Virgo A-Listers

Contemporary musicians and the Virgo award winners already named obviously qualify for the entertainment world's A list. In addition, these Virgo celebrities make headlines for just about anything they do.

Virgo A-Lister	Birthdate	Known for:
Quvenzhané Wallis	8/28/2003	Beasts of the Southern Wild
Blake Lively	8/25/1987	Gossip Girls
Lea Michele	8/29/1986	Glee
Nicole Richie	9/21/1981	Fashion consultant
Rachel Bilson	8/25/1981	Hart of Dixie
Michelle Williams	9/9/1980	Brokeback Mountain
Macaulay Culkin	8/26/1980	Home Alone movies
Alex O'Loughlin	8/24/1976	Hawaii Five-O
Jason Sudeikis	9/18/1975	Saturday Night Live
Jimmy Fallon	9/19/1974	Late night talk show
Idris Elba	9/6/1972	Luther
Cameron Diaz	8/30/1972	Movies

Jada Pinkett Smith	9/18/1971	Hawthorne; movies
Amy Poehler	9/16/1971	Parks and Recreation
David Arquette	9/8/1971	Scream movie series
Taraji Henson	9/11/1970	Person of Interest
Padma Lakshmi	9/1/1970	Top Chef
Melissa McCarthy	8/26/1970	Mike & Molly
Tyler Perry	9/13/1969	Madea series
Jack Black	8/28/1969	Bernie
Jason Priestley	8/28/1969	Beverly Hills 90210
Chandra Wilson	8/27/1969	Grey's Anatomy
Rachael Ray	8/25/1968	Cooking show host
Salma Hayek	9/2/1966	Frida
Charlie Sheen	9/3/1965	Two and a Half Men
Keanu Reeves	9/2/1964	Speed, The Matrix
Michael Chiklis	8/30/1963	Vegas
Mario Batali	9/9/1960	Italian cuisine
Hugh Grant	9/9/1960	Four Weddings and a Funeral
Jeff Foxworthy	9/6/1958	Are You Smarter Than a 5th Grader?
Michael Emerson	9/7/1954	Person of Interest
Mickey Rourke	9/16/1952	The Wrestler
Mark Harmon	9/2/1951	NCI
Phil McGraw	9/1/1950	#1 daytime talk show host
Richard Gere	8/31/1949	Pretty Woman
Lauren Bacall	9/16/1924	Classic movies

All about simplifying, really good living, affordable fashion, accessibility and sharing . . .

Rachael Ray, born 8/25/1968,
describing her show

Virgo Creativity Starters

- Criticize, but subtly
- Play with words
- Make a mystery to be solved
- Perfect a unique technique
- Rhyme
- Get grotesque

Sports

- Virgo Sports Glimpses
- Sports Birthday Calendar
- No Pains, No Gains
- Intellect
- Longevity
- Team Orientation

Virgo Sports Glimpses: Disciplined and Detailed

- Breakthrough techniques from snowboarder Shaun White (9/3/1986)
- Golfer Brittany Lincicome (9/19/1985) with another long drive
- Spectacular skating and puckhandling skills from Alexander Ovechkin (9/17/1985)
- Pitch variety for Olympic Gold from softballer Jennie Finch (9/3/1980)
- Kobe Bryant (8/23/1978) still averaging 25+ points and 5+ assists per game
- Olympic records from track stars Michael Johnson (9/13/1967), Edwin Moses (8/31/1955) and Jesse Owens (9/12/1913)

- The "Iron Man" work ethic of Cal Ripken Jr. (8/24/1960)
- 59-year-old golfer Tom Watson (9/4/1949) leading the British Open through three rounds
- Baseball manager Lou Piniella (8/28/1943) tossing a base after getting thrown out of a game
- Absolute team discipline from football coaches Tom Landry (9/11/1924) and Bear Bryant (9/11/1913)

Sports Birthday Calendar

Code	Sport / Role	Code	Sport / Role	Code	Sport / Role
A	Announcer	FS	Figure skating	SC	Soccer
AR	Auto racing	G	Golf	SF	Softball
BB	Baseball	GY	Gymnastics	SK	Alpine skiing
BK	Basketball	H	Hockey	SW	Swimming
BX	Boxing	HT	Horse trainer	T	Tennis
C	Coach	L	Luge	TF	Track and field
CY	Cycling	MC	Mountain climbing	W	Wrestling
DN	Dance	SA	Sailing		
F	Football	SB	Snowboarding		

August 23		Sport
1929	Peter Thomson	G
1934	Sonny Jurgensen	F
1978	Kobe Bryant	BK
1982	Natalie Coughlin	SW
1988	Jeremy Lin	BK

August 24		Sport
1890	Duke Kahanamoku	SW
1952	Mike Shanahan	F-C
1955	Hank Haney	G-C
1960	Cal Ripken Jr.	BB

August 25		Sport
1927	Althea Gibson	T
1946	Rollie Fingers	BB
1969	Catriona Matthew	G
1972	Marvin Harrison	F

1965	Reggie Miller	BK			
1970	Rich Beem	G			
1986	Arian Foster	F			

August 26		**Sport**	**August 27**		**Sport**
1985	David Price	BB	1957	Bernhard Langer	G
			1970	Jim Thome	BB
			1974	José Vidro	BB
			1987	Darren McFadden	F

August 28		**Sport**	**August 29**		**Sport**
1932	Andy Bathgate	H	1901	Aurele Joliat	H
1943	Lou Piniella	BB-C	1946	Bob Beamon	TF
1958	Scott Hamilton	FS	1958	Michael Jackson	DN
1964	Lee Janzen	G	1977	Roy Oswalt	BB
1971	Janet Evans	SW			

August 30		**Sport**	**August 31**		**Sport**
1918	Ted Williams	BB	1931	Jean Béliveau	H
1943	Jean-Claude Killy	SK	1935	Frank Robinson	BB-C
1978	Cliff Lee	BB	1955	Edwin Moses	TF
1982	Andy Roddick	T	1971	Padraig Harrington	G
			1973	Scott Niedermayer	H
			1983	Larry Fitzgerald	F
			1984	Charl Schwartzel	G
			1987	Sun-Ju Ahn	G

September 1		**Sport**	**September 2**		**Sport**
1923	Rocky Marciano	BX	1901	Adolph Rupp	BK-C
1962	Ruud Gullit	SC	1935	D. Wayne Lukas	HT
1973	Zach Thomas	F	1941	John Thompson	BK-C
1974	Jason Taylor	F	1948	Nate Archibald	BK
1981	Clinton Portis	F	1948	Terry Bradshaw	F-A
1986	Gael Monfils	T	1952	Jimmy Connors	T
			1960	Eric Dickerson	F

			1965	Lennox Lewis	BX
			1971	Kjetil Aamodt	SK
			1979	Alexander Povetkin	BX
			1987	Scott Moir	FS

September 3		**Sport**	**September 4**		**Sport**
1967	Luis Gonzalez	BB	1937	Dawn Fraser	SW
1977	Casey Hampton	F	1942	Raymond Floyd	G
1980	Jennie Finch	SF	1949	Tom Watson	G
1986	Shaun White	SB	1968	Mike Piazza	BB

September 5		**Sport**	**September 6**		**Sport**
1874	Nap Lajoie	BB	1974	Tim Henman	T
1936	Bill Maseroski	BB	1976	Brendon Ayanbadejo	F
1960	Willie Gault	TF-F			

September 7		**Sport**	**September 8**		**Sport**
1908	Paul Brown	F-C	1915	Duffy Daugherty	F
1910	Lee Wallard	AR	1951	Tim Gullikson	T-C
1923	Louise Suggs	G	1970	Latrell Sprewell	BK
1971	Briana Scurry	SC	1971	Brooke Burke	DN
1984	Vera Zvonareva	T			

September 9		**Sport**	**September 10**		**Sport**
1949	John Curry	FS	1929	Arnold Palmer	G
1949	Joe Theismann	F	1934	Roger Maris	BB
1966	Georg Hackl	L	1947	Larry Nelson	G
			1948	Bob Lanier	F
			1963	Randy Johnson	BB
			1974	Ben Wallace	BK
			1976	Gustavo Kuerten	T
			1983	Joey Votto	BB

September 11		**Sport**	**September 12**		**Sport**
1913	Bear Bryant	F-C	1913	Jesse Owens	TF
1924	Tom Landry	F-C	1949	Irina Rodnina	FS

1945	Franz Beckenbauer	SC	1969	Angel Cabrera	G
1957	Jeff Sluman	G	1975	Luis Castillo	BB
1978	Ed Reed	F	1976	José Théodore	H
1980	Mike Comrie	H	1980	Yao Ming	BK
			1989	Andrew Luck	F

September 13		**Sport**	**September 14**		**Sport**
1942	Bela Karolyi	GY-C	1886	Stanley Ketchel	BX
1967	Michael Johnson	TF	1940	Larry Brown	BK-C
1968	Bernie Williams	BB	1974	Hicham El Guerrouj	TF
1976	José Théodore	H	1987	Michael Crabtree	F
1989	Thomas Mueller	SC			

September 15		**Sport**	**September 16**		**Sport**
1936	Ashley Cooper	T	1934	Elgin Baylor	BK
1938	Gaylord Perry	BB	1943	Dennis Conner	SA
1940	Merlin Olsen	F	1955	Robin Yount	BB
1951	Pete Carroll	F-C	1958	Orel Hershiser	BB
1961	Dan Marino	F			
1979	Patrick Marleau	H			
1982	Aaron Ross	F			

September 17		**Sport**	**September 18**		**Sport**
1927	George Blanda	F	1905	Agnes de Mille	DN
1934	Maureen Connolly	T	1933	Scotty Bowman	H-C
1938	LeeRoy Yarbrough	AR	1952	Rick Pitino	BK-C
1944	Reinhold Messner	MC	1959	Ryne Sandberg	BB
1945	Phil Jackson	BK-C	1971	Lance Armstrong	CY
1974	Rasheed Wallace	BK	1976	Ronaldo	SC
1975	Jimmie Johnson	AR			
1980	Dan Haren	BB			
1985	Tomas Berdych	T			
1985	Alexander Ovechkin	H			

September 19		Sport	September 20		Sport
1922	Willie Pep	BX	1917	Red Auerbach	BK-C
1943	Joe Morgan	BB-A	1951	Guy Lafleur	H
1967	Alexander Karelin	W	1975	Juan Montoya	AR
1985	Brittany Lincicome	G	1978	Jason Bay	BB

September 21		Sport	September 22		
1953	Arie Luyendyk	AR	1927	Tommy Lasorda	BB-C
1983	Greg Jennings	F	1932	Ingemar Johansson	BX
1984	Dwayne Bowe	F			

No Pains, No Gains

The phrase "No Pains, No Gains" comes from the title of a poem by Robert Herrick (8/24/1591). Virgo athletes diligently practice the basic skills of the chosen sport. You put in the training hours. Virgo discipline delivers top performers in the conditioning-dependent sports of cycling, swimming, and track and field.

> *People ask me why I ride my bike for six hours a day; what is the pleasure? The answer is that I don't do it for the pleasure. I do it for the pain. In my most painful moments on the bike I am at my most self-aware and self-defining. That pain is temporary. It may last a minute, an hour, a day or a year, but eventually it subsides. And when it does, something else takes its place, and that thing might be called a greater space for happiness. Each time we overcome pain, I believe we grow.*
>
> Lance Armstrong, born 9/18/1971

> *How many years you have to keep on doing,*
> *until you know what to do and how to do!*
>
> Goethe, born 8/28/1749

Labor . . . is any painful exertion of mind or body undergone partly or wholly with a view to future good.
William Jevons, born 9/1/1835

You can be an ordinary athlete by getting away with less than your best. But if you want to be a great, you have to give it all you've got—your everything.
Olympic swimmer Duke Kahanamoku, born 8/24/1890

People always told me that my natural ability and good eyesight were the reasons for my success as a hitter. They never talk about the practice, practice, practice.
Ted Williams, born 8/30/1918

Most of us who aspire to be tops in our fields don't really consider the amount of work required to stay tops.
Althea Gibson, born 8/25/1927

You hit home runs not by chance, but by preparation.
Roger Maris, born 9/10/1934

Attention to detail instills pride and discipline.
D. Wayne Lukas, born 9/2/1935

Racing is an art form . . . I'm not there to hear the crowd yelling or to achieve glory or to earn money. I'm there to ski a perfect race.
Jean-Claude Killy, born 8/30/1943

I am not a very superstitious person. I don't go in for rabbit feet or garlic cloves or lucky pennies or any of that. To me, luck is work, preparation, ability, attitude, confidence, skill.
Dennis Conner, born 9/16/1943

My golf swing is like ironing a shirt. You get one side smoothed out, turn it over and there is a big wrinkle on the other side. You iron that side, turn it over and there's another wrinkle.

Tom Watson, born 9/4/1949

My confidence is in knowing that I have probably trained harder than anyone I am going to run against.

Michael Johnson, born 9/13/1967

Virgo Specialty: Track Stars

Virgo training discipline developed the zodiac's most impressive list of track superstars.

- Hicham El Guerrouj (9/14/1974) won two Olympic Golds and holds three world-record times for middle-distance running
- Michael Johnson (9/13/1967) remains the only male winner of 200-meter and 400-meter sprints in the same Olympics
- Edwin Moses (8/31/1955) won 400-meter hurdle Olympic Gold in 1976 and 1984
- Bob Beamon (8/29/1946) shattered the existing long jump record with a record that stood for 24 years
- Sprinter Jesse Owens (9/12/1913) set three world records in one day at the 1936 Berlin Olympics

A lifetime of training for just ten seconds.

Jesse Owens, born 9/12/1913

I'm often asked how I won 122 consecutive 400-meter hurdles races between 1977 and 1987. The answer is an unbreakable focus on disciplined training, executed with total dedication. My sole objective was to always be in top condition, to reach my desired level of concentration and performance at all times.

Training like that isn't glamorous, especially when it's sustained for almost a decade. It's difficult.

Edwin Moses, born 8/31/1955

Intellect

Thorough Virgo dissects the technical, mental and team components of sports success. Virgo athletes consciously develop the capacity for extended concentration. You are more likely than impetuous Aries or scattered Sagittarius to sustain the focus for repeat wins.

There is only a half-step difference between the champions and those who finish on the bottom. And much of that half step is mental.

Tom Landry, born 9/11/1924

The secret of concentration is the secret of self-discovery. You reach inside yourself to discover your personal resources, and what it takes to match them to the challenge.

Arnold Palmer, born 9/10/1929

Concentration is why some athletes are better than others. You develop that concentration in training. You can't be lackadaisical in training and concentrate in a meet.

Edwin Moses, born 8/31/1955

No one processes more information on every pitch than Ripken. He knows how batters hit depending on the count, the pitcher, the type of pitch and how they've been swinging in recent games. With his back to the infield, Ripken can tell where to throw a relay from the outfield by the sound of the crowd. He knows the very few managers in the league who will hit-and-run when their team is behind.

about Cal Ripken Jr., born 8/24/1960
Sports Illustrated

I don't want the other team to see me upset,
because I like to win the psychological battle
in a game. Being ice cold is the way I do it.

Briana Scurry, born 9/7/1971

These young guys are playing checkers.
I'm out there playing chess.

Kobe Bryant, born 8/23/1978

I think studying architecture and engineering you
study angles and space. This helps you in football.

Andrew Luck, born 9/12/1989

Virgo Specialty: Revered Coaches

Leo contributes flamboyant coaches like Bill Parcells and Nick Bollettieri, while Libra provides the gracious coaches like Tony Dungy and Joe Girardi. Virgo detail and team orientation combine to make the zodiac's longest list of legendary coaches revered by players and fans alike. Virgos who built championship dynasties by instilling long-term team discipline include Bear Bryant, Tom Landry, Scotty Bowman, John Thompson and Phil Jackson.

Virgo Coach	Birthdate	Best-known Coaching Position
Hank Haney	8/24/1955	Tiger Woods swing coach
Rick Pitino	9/18/1952	College basketball
Mike Shanahan	8/24/1952	Denver football, 2 Super Bowls
Pete Carroll	9/15/1951	Seattle football
Tim Gullikson	9/8/1951	Pete Sampras tennis mentor
Phil Jackson	9/17/1945	Chicago basketball
Lou Piniella	8/28/1943	Baseball
Bela Karolyi	9/13/1942	Olympic gymnasts
John Thompson	9/2/1941	Georgetown University basketball
Larry Brown	9/14/1940	NBA
Frank Robinson	8/31/1935	Washington Nationals
Scotty Bowman	9/18/1933	9 Stanley Cups
Tommy Lasorda	9/22/1927	Los Angeles baseball, Olympics
Tom Landry	9/11/1924	Dallas football, 2 Super Bowls
Red Auerbach	9/20/1917	Celtics basketball, 9 NBA titles
Duffy Daugherty	9/8/1915	Michigan State football
Bear Bryant	9/11/1913	Alabama football
Paul Brown	9/7/1908	Cleveland Browns football
Adolph Rupp	9/2/1901	4 NCAA basketball championships

Of all the mistakes a coach can make, I think one of the worst is to fall in love with the sound of his own voice. When I see a coach waving his clip board, furiously drawing diagrams, I see a coach who's selling himself to the TV cameras, selling himself to the crowd, when what he should be doing is selling his team.

Red Auerbach, born 9/20/1917

Wisdom is always an overmatch for strength.

Phil Jackson, born 9/17/1945

Longevity

Virgo's rigorous training helps your body execute for an extended period of time. Your hard-earned mental focus keeps you making the right decisions on the sports field. "Iron Man" Cal Ripken Jr. (8/24/1960) started 2,632 consecutive MLB games across 17 seasons, a record now considered virtually unbreakable. Virgo claims the zodiac's most impressive collection of sports longevity records.

Perseverance is based on two components: effort and desire. You've got to really want to do something to get by the rough spots, and you have to be willing to put the effort in. I always wanted to play baseball, and I've worked hard at it. I've had slumps. And for me a slump was always a big deal because of The Streak. People would say I'd played too much, I needed rest, I was hurting the team. It was difficult, but I'd just work harder. If my hitting was off, I'd go into the batting cage and try to hone in on the problem. It was very calming to work hard and sweat hard and repeat the motions until hitting came naturally again. I had to dig deep and work at it.

Cal Ripken Jr., born 8/24/1960

A gamer comes to the ballpark ready to meet the challenges of the day, no matter how difficult they are . . . I stuck to that mentality throughout my career, and it's the chief reason I was able to play 2,632 games in a row.

Cal Ripken Jr., born 8/24/1960

In sports, you simply aren't considered a real champion until you have defended your title successfully. Winning it once can be a fluke; winning it twice proves you are the best.

Althea Gibson, born 8/25/1927

I think I have proved I can sustain that high level of excellence, and I believe we're going to be this good for a long time.

D. Wayne Lukas, born 9/2/1935

I just try to be myself, whatever that is. I don't think about how I'll be remembered. I just want to be consistent over a long period of time. That's what the great players do.

Dan Marino, born 9/15/1961

Edwin Moses [Virgo born 8/31/1955]. He was a workaholic and I was a workaholic. He stayed around so long and was still graceful.

Reggie Miller, born 8/24/1965,
asked what athlete reminds him of himself

As long as it's still fun, which it still is, as long as I'm still passionate, which I still am, and as long as I am still competitive, which I hope to be, then I'll be around.

Lance Armstrong, born 9/18/1971

I was pretty good for a long time. For 13 or 14 years I was invested fully, every day. I've been pretty good about keeping my nose to the grindstone, I won a lot of matches from hard work and persistence.

Andy Roddick, born 8/30/1982,
asked what he was most proud of

Virgo Specialty: Consistency Records

- Lance Armstrong (9/18/1971) won seven consecutive Tour de France cycling races before his victories were disqualified
- Jim Thome (8/27/1970) continued hitting major league home runs into his 40s

- Cal Ripken Jr. (8/24/1960) started a record 2,632 consecutive baseball games
- Orel Hershiser (9/16/1958) pitched a record 59 consecutive scoreless innings
- Edwin Moses (8/31/1955) won 122 consecutive 400-meter hurdle races
- Jimmy Connors (9/2/1952) has won more tennis matches than any other male player in the open era
- At age 59, golfer Tom Watson (9/4/1949) lost the British Open in a playoff
- Baseball pitcher Gaylord Perry (9/15/1938) had 13 consecutive 15-win seasons
- Tommy Lasorda (9/22/1927) worked a record six decades in some capacity for Dodgers baseball
- George Blanda (9/17/1927) played professional football for a record 26 seasons
- Ted Williams (8/30/1918) held baseball's on-base percentage record for 61 years

The 1991 U.S. Open was the best 11 days of my career. To have been off for a year and have had my wrist reconstructed—nobody realized what I'd gone through to get back.

Jimmy Connors, born 9/2/1952

Team Orientation

Leo dreams of personal heroics, but Virgo doesn't need to be the star. You simply want to contribute to the team. Virgo tends to collaboration in all fields of endeavor.

First there are those who are winners, and know they are winners. Then there are the losers who know they are losers. Then there are those who are not winners, but don't know it. They're the ones for me. They never quit trying. They're the soul of our game.

Bear Bryant, born 9/11/1913

Once a player becomes bigger than the team, you no longer have a team.

Red Auerbach, born 9/20/1917

A team that has character doesn't need stimulation.

Tom Landry, born 9/11/1924

The emphasis should be on the team. There have been times during the streak when the emphasis was on the streak. I was never comfortable with that. It was time to move the focus back to the team.

Cal Ripken Jr., born 8/24/1960,
after taking himself out of line-up to end streak

In my 20s I thought, "I'm not the guy that's gonna have 25 years of hits." Producing and songwriting [for others] are more fun and rewarding. I just want to be on the team. I don't have to be in the starting lineup. And the way I keep my jersey is I collaborate.

Richard Marx, born 9/16/1963

I love my teammates. We embrace one another. We support each other.

Bernie Williams, born 9/13/1968

Americans don't understand that cycling is a team sport. They see a guy on a bike, they think: individual sport. At times it is. But I could never, ever win the Tour de France without the team. Never.

Lance Armstrong, born 9/18/1971

I don't consider myself as the best player in the world. I'm not obsessed with individual titles. I'm much more interested in being part of a team which wins trophies.

Ronaldo, born 9/18/1976

I'll do whatever it takes to win games, whether it's sitting on a bench waving a towel, handing a cup of water to a teammate, or hitting the game-winning shot.

Kobe Bryant, born 8/23/1978

I do my job on the mound and then do what I can at the plate, always working on helping the team anyway I can.

Jennie Finch, born 9/3/1980

It's not about how good you are; it's how good you are to work with.

Jennifer Hudson, born 9/12/1981

I would like to think I'm a good team player, put the team in a position to succeed and don't detract from anybody else on the team while lifting everybody up. It's a team game. The quarterback's gonna get the attention, but maybe it's not so deserving all the time.

Andrew Luck, born 9/12/1989

Virgo Football

These Virgo football stars appear on various lists of the greatest all-time football players. The Virgo list skews to quarterbacks and other on-field thinkers.

Football Legend	Birthdate	Best-known Position
Marvin Harrison	8/25/1972	Indianapolis receiver
Dan Marino	9/15/1961	Miami quarterback
Eric Dickerson	9/2/1960	LA / Indianapolis running back
Joe Theismann	9/9/1949	Washington quarterback
Terry Bradshaw	9/2/1948	Pittsburgh quarterback
Merlin Olsen	9/15/1940	LA Rams defensive end
Sonny Jurgensen	8/23/1934	Washington quarterback
George Blanda	9/17/1927	Oakland quarterback and kicker

I worked hard. I worked late. I went in early. I did everything I could to gain an advantage.

Joe Theismann

Contemporary Virgo football stars are selected from top fantasy football rankings and recent Pro Bowl appearances. (Go to www.QuotableZodiac.com for astrological updates on all 21st-century sports stars.)

Football All-Star	Birthdate	Best-known Position
Andrew Luck	9/12/1989	Indianapolis quarterback
Michael Crabtree	9/14/1987	San Francisco receiver
Darren McFadden	8/27/1987	Oakland running back
Arian Foster	8/24/1986	Houston running back
Dwayne Bowe	9/21/1984	Kansas City receiver
Greg Jennings	9/21/1983	Green Bay receiver
Larry Fitzgerald	8/31/1983	Arizona receiver
Ed Reed	9/11/1978	Baltimore safety
Brendon Ayanbadejo	9/6/1976	Special teams all-star

In college, most of the time you can get by on your athletic ability. Sometimes last year, I got by on athletic ability. But it only takes you so far. To be an upper-echelon receiver in the league? You've got to be consistent on a daily basis in route running.

Larry Fitzgerald

Virgo Specialty: #2 in Baseball Stars

Consistent Virgo places second to Taurus in baseball legends. Most all-time baseball lists include the following Virgos:

Baseball Legend	Birthdate	Known for:
Jim Thome	8/27/1970	#7 all-time home runs
Randy Johnson	9/10/1963	Strikeouts
Cal Ripken Jr.	8/24/1960	2,632 consecutive games
Ryne Sandberg	9/18/1959	9 consecutive Golden Gloves (2nd base)
Orel Hershiser	9/16/1958	World Series MVP
Robin Yount	9/16/1955	3,142 hits
Joe Morgan	9/19/1943	2 World Series wins (2nd base)
Gaylord Perry	9/15/1938	Cy Young in each league
Bill Maseroski	9/5/1936	Only homer to win World Series game 7
Frank Robinson	8/31/1935	American and National League MVP
Roger Maris	9/10/1934	61 home runs (single season)
Ted Williams	8/30/1918	Last batting average > .400
Nap Lajoie	9/5/1874	Hitting; Triple Crown

There are a lot of stories told about how I cared for my bats, weighed them, knew if they were a little too heavy or a little too light—usually they'd get a little too heavy. They're pretty much true. I did take care of my bats. Bone them down. Make sure they didn't take on extra weight. Hell, an extra half-ounce from dirt or moisture can make a big difference in your swing. How fast you get around. Where you make contact. Where the ball goes.

Ted Williams

In addition to Thome, Ripken and Randy Johnson, baseball fans voted these contemporary Virgo players to Major League Baseball's all-star roster on at least three occasions. At least one all-star appearance fell in the 21st century.

Baseball All-Star	Birthdate	Best-known Position
David Price	8/26/1985	Tampa Bay pitcher
Joey Votto	9/10/1983	Cincinnati first base
Dan Haren	9/17/1980	Pitcher
Jason Bay	9/20/1978	Pittsburgh outfielder
Cliff Lee	8/30/1978	Pitcher
Roy Oswalt	8/29/1977	Houston pitcher
Luis Castillo	9/12/1975	Florida second base
José Vidro	8/27/1974	Second base
Bernie Williams	9/13/1968	NY Yankee outfield
Mike Piazza	9/4/1968	Los Angeles catcher
Luis Gonzalez	9/3/1967	Arizona outfielder

I can't blow the ball by guys. I have to pitch. I have to outthink guys.

Dan Haren

Virgo Basketball

This list includes Virgos typically named to all-time basketball player lists and those earning NBA Most Valuable Player honors.

Basketball Legend	Birthdate	Best-known Position
Kobe Bryant	8/23/1978	Los Angeles scorer
Nate Archibald	9/2/1948	Kansas City / Boston point guard
Elgin Baylor	9/16/1934	Los Angeles forward

In addition to Kobe Bryant, these Virgos earned at least three recent appearances in the NBA's annual All-Star game.

Basketball Player	Birthdate	Best-known Position
Yao Ming	9/12/1980	Houston center
Rasheed Wallace	9/17/1974	Portland / Detroit power forward
Ben Wallace	9/10/1974	Detroit center
Latrell Sprewell	9/8/1970	Shooting guard / small forward
Reggie Miller	8/24/1965	Indiana shooting guard

We don't see ourselves as four All-Stars.
We see ourselves as one unit. It's like five
fingers on a hand. You can do more damage
together as a fist than spread out flat.

Rasheed Wallace

Virgo Specialty: #2 in Hockey MVP Awards

With your team orientation and skating and shooting skills, Virgo trails only innovative Aquarius in professional hockey Most Valuable Player awards.

Hockey Player	Birthdate	Best-known Position
Alexander Ovechkin (2x)	9/17/1985	Washington scorer
José Théodore	9/13/1976	Montreal goalie
Guy Lafleur (2x)	9/20/1951	Montreal winger (5 Stanley Cups)
Andy Bathgate	8/28/1932	New York center
Jean Béliveau (2x)	8/31/1931	Montreal center (10 Stanley Cups)
Aurele Joliat	8/29/1901	Montreal forward

I think it was always there and it was maybe a matter of bringing it out. It was harder than I thought it would be and I had to try harder. I had to regain my confidence, maybe the most important thing. I have learned a lot to relax. I know what I can do now, and I do it.

Guy Lafleur about returning to the NHL after retirement

In addition to Ovechkin, these Virgo players earned at least three recent appearances in professional hockey's annual All-Star game.

Hockey All-Star	Birthdate	Best-known Position
Patrick Marleau	9/15/1979	San Jose forward
Scott Niedermayer	8/31/1973	New Jersey defense

Virgo Soccer

Soccer Player	Birthdate	Nationality and Position
Thomas Mueller	9/13/1989	German "Golden Boot"
Ronaldo	9/18/1976	Brazilian scorer (World Cup record)
Briana Scurry	9/7/1971	USA goalie
Ruud Gullit	9/1/1962	Versatile Dutch player and manager
Franz Beckenbauer	9/11/1945	World Cup as German player, manager

I love to score goals after passing all the defenders as well as the keeper. This is not my specialty, but my habit.

Ronaldo

Virgo Olympians

Virgo provides these famous Olympic athletes in addition to the track stars already listed. Virgo Olympians skew to lengthy careers and training-intensive sports.

Virgo Athlete	Birthdate	Country	Known for:
Scott Moir	9/2/1987	Canada	Ice dance Gold
Shaun White	9/3/1986	USA	2 halfpipe Golds
Natalie Coughlin	8/23/1982	USA	12 swimming medals
Jennie Finch	9/3/1980	USA	Dominant softball pitcher
Kjetil Aamodt	9/2/1971	Norway	8 alpine ski medals
Janet Evans	8/28/1971	USA	4 distance swimming Golds
Alexander Karelin	9/19/1967	Russia	Wrestling medals, 4 consecutive Games

Georg Hackl	9/9/1966	Germany	Luge medals, 5 consecutive Games
Scott Hamilton	8/28/1958	USA	Figure skating Gold
Irina Rodnina	9/12/1949	Soviet Union	3 consecutive pairs skating Golds
Jean-Claude Killy	8/30/1943	France	Triple alpine ski Gold
Dawn Fraser	9/4/1937	Australia	3 consecutive swim sprint Golds

The whole sexiness thing—I don't know if I'm comfortable with that. But it has helped the sport grow. I think it changes how people see women's athletics.

Jennie Finch

Virgo Specialty: #2 in Golf Champions

The list of Virgo golf champions includes only those Virgos who have won at least two majors. Women's majors include the British Open, U.S. Open, LPGA Championship, Kraft and several earlier events that have since been de-emphasized. Only four women's major championships have been held each year. The men's major championships are the British Open, U.S. Open, PGA Championship and The Masters.

Golf Champion	Birthdate	Country	# Majors
Louise Suggs	9/7/1923	USA	11
Tom Watson	9/4/1949	USA	8
Arnold Palmer	9/10/1929	USA	7
Peter Thomson	8/23/1929	Australia	5
Raymond Floyd	9/4/1942	USA	4
Padraig Harrington	8/31/1971	Ireland	3
Larry Nelson	9/10/1947	USA	3
Angel Cabrera	9/12/1969	Argentina	2
Lee Janzen	8/28/1964	USA	2
Bernhard Langer	8/27/1957	Germany	2

A game in which you claim the privileges of age, and retain the playthings of childhood.
Samuel Johnson, born 9/18/1709

Golf is deceptively simple, endlessly complicated. A child can play it well and a grown man can never master it. It is almost a science, yet it is a puzzle with no answers.
Arnold Palmer, born 9/10/1929

Golf Contender	Birthdate	Country
Sun-Ju Ahn	8/31/1987	South Korea
Brittany Lincicome	9/19/1985	USA
Charl Schwartzel	8/31/1984	South Africa
Catriona Matthew	8/25/1969	Scotland

Virgo Tennis

The tennis champions list includes only those Virgos who have won at least three major championships since 1950. Major tennis events are Wimbledon, the Australian Open, the French Open and the U.S. Open.

Tennis Champion	Birthdate	Country	# Majors
Maureen Connolly	9/17/1934	USA	9
Jimmy Connors	9/2/1952	USA	8
Althea Gibson	8/25/1927	USA	5
Ashley Cooper	9/15/1936	Australia	4
Gustavo Kuerten	9/10/1976	Brazil	3

I don't know that my behavior has improved that much with age. They just found someone worse.
Jimmy Connors

I think it was the top achievement of my career. To win the way I did there, playing the final the way I did against Andre in a very precise way, almost a perfect match. It was the toughest performance I ever had.

Gustavo Kuerten

Tennis Contender	Birthdate	Country
Gael Monfils	9/1/1986	France
Tomas Berdych	9/17/1985	Czech Republic
Vera Zvonareva	9/7/1984	Russia

Virgo Boxing

Boxer	Birthdate	Known for:
Alexander Povetkin	9/2/1979	WBA heavyweight champ
Lennox Lewis	9/2/1965	Undisputed world heavyweight champ
Ingemar Johansson	9/22/1932	Powerful Swedish heavyweight champ
Rocky Marciano	9/1/1923	Untied, undefeated champ
Willie Pep	9/19/1922	26-year featherweight career
Stanley Ketchel	9/14/1886	One of the greatest middleweight champs

In boxing you create a strategy to beat each new opponent, it's just like chess.

Lennox Lewis

Virgo Dance

Virgo Dancer	Birthdate	Known for:
Brooke Burke	9/8/1971	Dancing With the Stars
Michael Jackson	8/29/1958	Moonwalk
Agnes de Mille	9/18/1905	Emotional choreography

I'm not one of the gang. Never have been. That was always the trouble. A woman has to be seductive, flirty, lovely, clever. I was busy, harassed, not attractive. Attractive means time and energy and I didn't give attractiveness time. I was told that I had no sex appeal. But when I got on stage, I got yells of laughter. And I could make an audience cry.

Agnes de Mille, born 9/18/1905

Virgo Auto Racing

Here are the Virgo winners of the Daytona 500, the Indy 500 (since 1946), and the NASCAR series now called the Sprint Cup.

Virgo Driver	Birthdate	Event(s) Won
Juan Montoya	9/20/1975	Indy 500
Jimmie Johnson	9/17/1975	Daytona 500 (2x), Sprint Cup (5x)
Arie Luyendyk	9/21/1953	Indy 500 (2x)
LeeRoy Yarbrough	9/17/1938	Daytona 500
Lee Wallard	9/7/1910	Indy 500

I have a lot of confidence in myself, a lot of confidence
in the race team, our equipment and if my mind
plays games on me, I just fall back on the team.

Jimmie Johnson

Spirituality

God loves me. I'm not here just to fill a place, just to be a number. He has chosen me for a purpose. I know it.

Mother Teresa, born 8/26/1910

- **Service Orientation**
- **Asceticism**
- **Simple Devotion**

Virgo Religious Figures

Religious Figure	Birthdate	Known as:
James Van Praagh	8/23/1958	Spiritualist, mystic medium
Paulo Coelho	8/24/1947	Spiritual writer; The Alchemist
Robert Schuller	9/16/1926	Crystal Cathedral founder
Mother Teresa	8/26/1910	Help for the poor
Swami Sivananda	9/8/1887	Spiritual teacher, proponent of yoga
Lloyd Douglas	8/27/1877	Minister; The Robe novelist
Ralph Waldo Trine	9/6/1866	Philosopher, mystic
St. Elizabeth Seton	8/28/1774	Community care for poor children
Robert South	9/4/1634	English clergyman
Cardinal Richelieu	9/9/1585	Chief Minister of France

Service Orientation

If you can't feed a hundred people, then feed just one.
Mother Teresa, born 8/26/1910

Our job in life is to witness to the truth, not in any sense of vengeance or anger, but in standing up for the people who are being abused, who are suffering.
Richard Gere, born 8/31/1949

Capricorn and Virgo express spirituality through service. Capricorn develops service structures such as the American Red Cross and St. Jude's Children's Research Hospital. Virgos St. Elizabeth Seton and Mother Teresa lived among the poor, dedicating their lives to providing aid. Virgo's spiritual service stays in touch with the people.

It is our first duty to serve society, and, after we have done that, we may attend wholly to the salvation of our own souls. A youthful passion for abstracted devotion should not be encouraged.
Samuel Johnson, born 9/18/1709

This faith is not like a deed to a house in which one may live with full rights of possession. It is more like a kit of tools with which a man may build himself a house. The tools will be worth just what he does with them. When he lays them down, they will have no value until he takes them up again.
Lloyd Douglas, born 8/27/1877
The Robe

Should I devote myself to the struggle for justice
when the most needy people would die right
in front of me for lack of a glass of milk?

Mother Teresa, born 8/26/1910

These firefighters are true bodhisattvas. They save everyone. They don't ask, "Are you a good guy, a bad guy?" They don't care what your color is, what your religion is. They don't care if you have money or if you don't have money. If you're in trouble, they get you out. That's a bodhisattva.

Richard Gere, born 8/31/1949

Asceticism

In many ways I'm a monk already.

Richard Gere, born 8/31/1949

Disciplined Virgo is the monk of the zodiac. The Virgo tendencies to thorough thinking and personal retreat fit the communal routines of silence and contemplation. Physical privation trains your mind to obedience.

Abstinence is the great strengthener
and clearer of reason.

Robert South, born 9/4/1634

Abstinence is as easy for me as
temperance would be difficult.

Samuel Johnson, born 9/18/1709

It is in self-limitation that a master first shows himself.

Goethe, born 8/28/1749

Can there be virtue in penances suffered by the body to do away offenses of the soul? If there be!—O if there be, let them channel my body with stripes, and swathe round in one continued firth of wounds! Any thing that can be endured here is mercy compared to the dreadful abiding of what may be hereafter.

Joanna Baillie, born 9/11/1762
The Dream

A priest is he who lives solely in the realm
of the invisible, for whom all that is visible
has only the truth of an allegory.

August Schlegel, born 9/8/1767

Terrible is the fight put up by the senses.
Fight bravely! Conquer them you must.

Swami Sivananda, born 9/8/1887

Meditation is painful in the beginning but it bestows
immortal Bliss and supreme joy in the end.

Swami Sivananda, born 9/8/1887

Our teacher says that the nature of Helios is a secret
of the god; and that a man's first business is to know
himself, and seek the source of light in his own soul.

Mary Renault, born 9/4/1905
The Last of the Wine

To the world, it seems foolish that we delight in poor food, possess only three sets of habits made of coarse cloth, enjoy walking in any shape and color of shoes, bathe with just a bucket of water, go hungry and thirsty but refuse to eat in the houses of other people, walk distances in the rain and hot summer sun, travel third-class overcrowded trains, sleep on hard beds, kneel on the rough and thin carpets in the chapel, work like coolies at home and outside when we could easily employ servants and do

only the light jobs. To some we are wasting our precious life and burying our talents. Our beautiful work with and for the poor is a privilege and a gift to us.

Mother Teresa, born 8/26/1910

I started working on myself, began meditation,
exploring different teachers. I was always interested
in moral and metaphysical questions: What are the
underpinnings of reality? The mind? Where is the soul?

Richard Gere, born 8/31/1949

The spirit world is able to get through to you easily when your mind is still and clear. Meditation is often referred to as "sitting in the silence." Whenever you want to reach Spirit from this side of life, start by sitting in the silence.

James Van Praagh, born 8/23/1958

For everything to click, my weight and diet have to
be right, and I can't have any negative elements in
my life. Cyclists should live like monks: eat, sleep,
ride. My life's not like that now, but it used to be.

Lance Armstrong, born 9/18/1971

Virgo Tarot Card: The Hermit

Metaphysical tradition links Virgo to Tarot card IX, The Hermit. The hooded figure on the card uses a walking stick and holds up a lantern to light the way. The card indicates that inner contemplation is necessary to achieve the deeper gifts of Light. Celtic tradition identifies the figure on the card as Merlin, the spiritual guide who instructed and served King Arthur before retreating to private life.

And the lovely month came, September, my birth-month, the wind's month, the month of the raven, and of Myrrdin himself, that wayfarer between heaven and earth.

Mary Stewart, born 9/17/1916
The Last Enchantment (narrated by Merlin)

I was very anxious for him not to be one of those pointy-headed wizard guys. This is a guy who makes mistakes. And those errors were what I related to.

Sam Neill, born 9/14/1947,
about his role as Merlin

Simple Devotion

Virgo contemplation often concludes with a pure and simple faith in God. You accept direction from a higher power without asking why. You perceive your immediate surroundings as a microcosm of the infinite.

Put your heart at His feet. It is the gift He loves most.

St. Elizabeth Seton, born 8/28/1774

There is no greatness where there is not simplicity.

Leo Tolstoy, born 9/9/1828

A miracle is nothing more or less than this. Anyone who has come into a knowledge of his true identity, of his oneness with the all-pervading wisdom and power, this makes it possible for laws higher than the ordinary mind knows of to be revealed to him.

Ralph Waldo Trine, born 9/6/1866

The Goddess sat on the altar, in a little throne of painted wood. But she herself was stone. She was round and dimpled, both a woman and a stone . . . Waist she had none, being great with child; her small arms were folded between her great belly and heavy breasts, her huge thighs tapered to tiny feet. She was unpainted, unclothed, unjewelled; a small

round gray stone. There was no face to see; it was bowed upon her breasts, showing only rough-carved curls. Yet I shivered and sweated; she was so old, so old.

Mary Renault, born 9/4/1905
The Bull from the Sea

Christianity is a very simple thing: love other persons, as you love God. Be as perfect as your father in heaven. Live in the spirit of God, making the best things, in the best possible way, for the best purposes. Even a small child can understand these ideas, and even a great mind cannot improve upon them.

Theodore Parker, born 8/24/1910

God hasn't called me to be successful.
He's called me to be faithful.

Mother Teresa, born 8/26/1910

I happen to think that the great spirit God
made us all, put us all here for a reason.
And all of us have something to do.

B.B. King, born 9/16/1925

God's delays are not God's denials.

Robert Schuller, born 9/16/1926

I discovered the courage to write down my
prayers. To apply to the source of mercy.

Leonard Cohen, born 9/21/1934

If you want to hear God laugh, tell Him your plans.

Iyanla Vanzant, born 9/15/1953

Every situation—nay, every moment—is of infinite
worth; for it is the representative of a whole eternity.

Goethe, born 8/28/1749

Every second is of infinite value.
Joanna Baillie, born 9/11/1762

Put your heart, mind, intellect and soul even to your smallest acts. This is the secret of success.
Swami Sivananda, born 9/8/1887

You don't even have to understand the desert; all you have to do is contemplate a simple grain of sand, and you will see in it all the marvels of creation.
Paulo Coelho, born 8/24/1947
The Alchemist

The meaning of life is contained in every single expression of life. It is present in the infinity of forms and phenomena that exist in all of creation.
Michael Jackson, born 8/29/1958

A person should hear a little music, read a little poetry and see a fine picture every day in order that worldly cares do not obliterate the sense of the beautiful which God has implanted in the human soul.
Goethe, born 8/28/1749

Maturity

The crucial task of old age is balance: keeping just well enough, just brave enough, just gay and interested and starkly honest enough to remain a sentient human being.

Florida Scott-Maxwell, born 9/14/1883

- **Still a Virgo**
- **Mentally Sharp**
- **More Tolerant**
- **Calm**

Still a Virgo

I'm fifty-six and still a Virgo.

Liz Carpenter, born 9/1/1920

Aging Virgos continue to complain, criticize and gossip. Your basic instincts for neatness and precision have softened around the edges, but they're still there.

Old people love to give good advice; it compensates them for their inability to set a bad example.
François de La Rochefoucauld, born 9/15/1613

How prone are we to blame others, when we ourselves only are in fault.
Marguerite Blessington, 9/1/1789
The Confessions of an Elderly Lady

No matter how old a mother is, she watches her middle-aged children for signs of improvement.
Florida Scott-Maxwell, born 9/14/1883
The Measure of My Days

My kitchen linoleum is so black and shiny that I waltz while I wait for the kettle to boil. This pleasure is for the old who live alone. The others must vanish into their expected role.
Florida Scott-Maxwell, born 9/14/1883

Like an old wife at the cottage door, I have little else to do but observe my neighbors.
Mary Stewart, born 9/17/1916
The Last Enchantment

Boy, I thought Cobb was [critical] and here I'm getting older, and I find I'm more critical.
Ted Williams, born 8/30/1918

I'm a perfectionist. I need to be needed. I need to do things for a man. But I don't need to do them as much, these days.
Jacqueline Bisset, born 9/13/1944

I don't need you to remind me of my age.
I have a bladder to do that for me.
Stephen Fry, born 8/24/1957

Mentally Sharp

Virgo's brain stays alert and active as you mature. Your steady work habits lend career longevity, and many older Virgos choose to keep working. Now in his 80s, financial guru Warren Buffett (8/30/1930) continues wise investments and sage financial advice through changing economic times.

The young man knows the rules but the
old man knows the exceptions.
Oliver Wendell Holmes, born 8/29/1809

You stay young as long as you can learn,
acquire new habits and suffer contradiction.
Marie von Ebner-Eschenbach, born 9/13/1830

Keep interested in others; keep interested in
the wide and wonderful world. Then, in a
spiritual sense, you will always be young.
Fredric March, born 8/31/1897

As long as my health stays good, all I really want to do
is keep working. That seems to be what I'm here for.
Lauren Bacall, born 9/16/1924

One can learn, at least. One can go on
learning until the day one is cut off.
Fay Weldon, born 9/22/1931
Down Among the Women

There is a fountain of youth: it is your mind, your talents, the creativity you bring to your life and the lives of the people you love. When you learn to tap this source, you will have truly defeated age.

Sophia Loren, born 9/20/1934

It's never too late for older golfers to learn new tricks.

Tom Watson, born 9/4/1949

I'd get bored after a few weeks.
I'll be working until I die.

Joan Jett, born 9/22/1960,
about not retiring

I have enjoyed greatly the second blooming that comes when you finish the life of the emotions and of personal relations; and suddenly find—at the age of 50, say—that a whole new life has opened before you, filled with things you can think about, study, or read about . . . It is as if a fresh sap of ideas and thoughts was rising in you.

Agatha Christie, born 9/15/1890

Change excites me. At 50, the mind starts to catch up with the body.

Raquel Welch, born 9/5/1940

I think I'm pretty lucky because my job doesn't have mandatory retirement at 65. It's really sad that so many great people are forced to retire at a time when they can be really helpful, because I think we just get better.

B.B. King, born 9/16/1925

Go out in a field
And start right in to work: dig, hoe,
Keep your thoughts and yourself in that field,
Eat the food your raise, live with your beasts as a beast,
Be willing to manure the field you harvest,
And that's the best way—take it from me!—
To be on being young at eighty.

Goethe, born 8/28/1749
Faust

Ordinary people know little of the time and effort it takes to learn to read. I have been 80 years at it, and have not reached my goal.

Goethe, born 8/28/1749

I do it because I still get a kick out of it. I still love performing. It keeps me young.

80-year-old B.B. King, born 9/16/1925

Age puzzles me. I thought it was a quiet time. My 70s were interesting and fairly serene, but my 80s are passionate. I grow more intense as I age.

Florida Scott-Maxwell, born 9/14/1883

More Tolerant

The evolving Virgo develops tolerance. With increasing age, Virgo tempers the instinctive reactions of judgment and corrective comment.

When we do not find peace of mind in ourselves it is useless to look for it elsewhere.

François de La Rochefoucauld, born 9/15/1613

As I know more of mankind I expect less of them, and am ready now to call a man a good man upon easier terms than I was formerly.

Samuel Johnson, born 9/18/1709

Life teaches us to be less harsh with ourselves and with others.

Goethe, born 8/28/1749
Iphigenia in Tauris

Tolerance comes with age. I see no fault committed that I myself could not have committed at some time or another.

Goethe, born 8/28/1749

The learner always begins by finding fault, but the scholar sees the positive merit in everything.

Georg Hegel, born 8/27/1770

Today, the new being that I am realizes that it is no longer time for sarcasm and that the only thing I can bring to this illogical, irresponsible and cruel universe is my love.

Jean Renoir, born 9/15/1894

At one point, I was tempted to give up my home and go out and start proselytizing. I was scary self-righteous. Something had to give.

Moby, born 9/11/1965

Calm

You have worked hard over the years and you feel good about it. Virgo finds the rewards of calm and simplicity.

Sometimes I see things backward because I'm jumping ahead of everything. I'm realizing as I get older that, at some point, it becomes your own responsibility to slow yourself down.

Cameron Diaz, born 8/30/1972

One of the delights known to age, and beyond the grasp of youth, is that of "not going."

J.B. Priestley, born 9/13/1894

I still like me, inside and out. Not in a vain way—I just feel good in my skin.

Sophia Loren, born 9/20/1934, in her mid-50s

I look back on my life like a good day's work, it was done and I am satisfied with it.

Grandma Moses, born 9/7/1860

I am satisfied. I have done what I want to do.

75-year-old Agatha Christie, born 9/15/1890

Words to Live By

Rise with the hour for which you were made.
Georgia Douglas Johnson, born 9/10/1880

Be uncool. As uncool as you can possibly be.
Write to me about the result. Be hot.
Anna Deavere Smith, born 9/18/1950

The man who thinks his wife, his baby, his house,
his horse, his dog, and himself severely unequalled,
is almost sure to be a good-humored person.
Oliver Wendell Holmes, born 8/29/1809

Nothing is worth more than this day.
Goethe, born 8/28/1749

I don't live in either my past or my future. I'm interested only in the present. If you can concentrate always on the present, you'll be a happy man. You'll see that there is life in the desert, that there are stars in the heavens, and that tribesmen fight because they are part of the human race. Life will be a party for you, a grand festival, because life is the moment we're living right now.
Paulo Coelho, born 8/24/1947

I hope you will remember that who seeketh two strings to one bow, he may shoot strong but never straight.

Queen Elizabeth I, born 9/17/1533

Beware of dissipating your powers; strive constantly to concentrate them.

Goethe, born 8/28/1749

Nothing contributes so much to tranquilize the mind as a steady purpose—a point on which the soul may fix its intellectual eye.

Mary Shelley, born 8/30/1797

Any fool can be fussy and rid himself of energy all over the place, but a man has to have something in him before he can settle down to do nothing.

J.B. Priestley, born 9/13/1894

If you don't know where you are going, you will probably end up somewhere else.

Laurence Peter, born 9/16/1919

You don't get to a place without focusing on it somehow.

Richard Gere, born 8/31/1949

Knowing is not enough; we must apply. Willing is not enough; we must do.

Goethe, born 8/28/1749

I find the great thing in this world is not so much where we stand, as in what direction we are moving: To reach the port of heaven, we must sail sometimes with the wind and sometimes against it, but we must sail, and not drift, nor lie at anchor.

Oliver Wendell Holmes, born 8/29/1809

Life is what we make it. Always
has been, always will be.
Grandma Moses, born 9/7/1860

The happiest people are those who are too
busy to notice whether they are or not.
William Feather, born 8/25/1889

Success doesn't come to you. You go to it.
Marva Collins, born 8/31/1936

"There is only one way to learn," the alchemist
answered. "It's through action."
Paulo Coelho, born 8/24/1947

If you are idle, be not solitary; if
you are solitary, be not idle.
Samuel Johnson, born 9/18/1709

The strongest of all warriors are these
two—Time and Patience.
Leo Tolstoy, born 9/9/1828

We give advice, but we cannot give
the wisdom to profit by it.
François de La Rochefoucauld, born 9/15/1613

When any fit of gloominess, or perversion
of mind, lays hold upon you, make it a
rule not to publish it by complaints.
Samuel Johnson, born 9/18/1709

Men of genius are not quick judges of character. Deep thinking and high imagining blunt that trivial instinct by which you and I size people up.

Max Beerbohm, born 8/24/1872

For fast-acting relief, try slowing down.

Lily Tomlin, born 9/1/1937

The two words "information" and "communication" are often used interchangeably, but they signify quite different things. Information is giving out; communication is getting through.

Sydney Harris, born 9/14/1917

Worry less about what other people think about you, and more about what you think about them.

Fay Weldon, born 9/22/1931

My dad used to say, "You wouldn't worry so much about what people thought of you if you knew how seldom they did."

Phil McGraw, born 9/1/1950

People just want to be acknowledged. If you just take a second to acknowledge the individual, then everything would go so much better.

Phil McGraw, born 9/1/1950

If someone won't take you as you are, you don't need them in your life. Go on to somebody else. Chapter Two.

Faith Hill, born 9/21/1967

Whatever you can do,
or dream you can, begin it.
Boldness has genius, power, and magic in it.
Begin it now.

Goethe, born 8/28/1749

Selected Bibliography

Compiled and arranged by Abby Adams, *An Uncommon Scold*, Simon and Schuster, New York, 1989.

Amende, Coral, *Hollywood Confidential*, Plume (imprint of Dutton Sargent, div Penguin Books), New York, 1997.

Edited by John Bartlett and Justin Kaplan, *Bartlett's Familiar Quotations*, Little, Brown and Company, Boston, 1992.

Bergman, Ingrid and Alan Burgess, *My Story*, Delacorte Press, New York, 1980.

Broman, Sven, *Conversations with Greta Garbo*, Viking, New York, 1992.

Burt, Kathleen, *Archetypes of the Zodiac*, Llewellyn Worldwide Ltd., St. Paul, Minnesota, 1990.

Cady, Barbara, *Icons of the 20th Century*, The Overlook Press, Woodstock, New York, 1998.

Edited by James Charlton, *The Military Quotation Book*, Thomas Dunne Books (imprint of St. Martin's Press), New York, 2002.

Christie, Agatha, *An Autobiography*, Harper, New York, 1977.

Coelho, Paulo, *The Alchemist*, translated by Alan R. Clarke, HarperOne, New York, 1993.

Compiled and arranged by John Cook, *The Book of Positive Quotations*, Fairview Press, Minneapolis, Minnesota, 1993.

Deger, Steve, *The Boy's Book of Positive Quotations*, Fairview Press, Minneapolis, Minnesota, 2009.

De Vito, Carlo, *The Ultimate Dictionary of Sports Quotations*, Checkmark Books, New York, 2001.

Dingle, Carol A., *Memorable Quotations: Virgo Luminaries of the Past*, 2008.

Goethe, Johann Wolfgang von, *Faust*, translated by Randall Jarrell, Farrar, Straus and Giroux, New York, 1976.

Goldschneider, Gary, *The Secret Language of Relationships*, Penguin Studio, New York, 1997.

Goodman, Linda, *Linda Goodman's Sun Signs*, Bantam Books, New York, 1968.

Greene, Liz, *The Astrology of Fate*, Samuel Weiser Inc., York Beach, Maine, 1984.

Hellstern, Melissa, *Getting Along Famously*, Dutton (member of Penguin Group), New York, 2008.

Jackson, Gordon, S., *Never Scratch a Tiger with a Short Stick*, NavPress, Colorado Springs, 2003.

Jagendorf, M. A., *Stories and Lore of the Zodiac*, The Vanguard Press Inc., New York, 1977.

Edited by Elizabeth Knowles, *The Oxford Dictionary of Phrase, Saying, and Quotation*, Oxford University Press, New York, 1997.

Compiled by Glenn Liebman, *2,000 Sports Quips and Quotes*, Gramercy Books, New York, 1993.

Lowe, Janet, *Warren Buffett Speaks*, John Wiley & Sons Inc., New York, 1997.

Compiled by Rosalie Maggio, *The Beacon Book of Quotations by Women*, Beacon Press, Boston, 1992.

Compiled by J. Michael Mahoney, *Topsy Turvy*, AuthorHouse, Bloomington, Indiana, 2009.

Matthews, John and Caitlín, *The Element Encyclopedia of Magical Creatures*, HarperCollins Publishers, London, 2005.

Edited by Peter McWilliams, *The LIFE 101 Quote Book*, Prelude Press, Los Angeles, 1996.

Edited by John Miller and Aaron Kenedi, *lovers*, a Bulfinch Press Book, Little, Brown and Company, New York, 1999.

Oken, Alan, *Alan Oken's Complete Astrology*, Bantam Books, New York, 1988.

The Oxford Dictionary of Quotations, Oxford University Press, New York, 1979.

Compiled by Charles Panati, *Words to Live By*, Penguin Books, New York, 1999.

Parker, Derek and Julia, *Sun & Moon Signs*, DK Publishing Inc., New York, 1996.

Compiled and edited by Elaine Partnow, *The Quotable Woman From Eve to 1799*, Facts on File Publications, New York, 1985.

Pickering, David, *Cassell's Sports Quotations*, Cassell & Co, London, 2000.

Edited by Connie Robertson, *The Wordsworth Dictionary of Quotations*, Wordsworth Editions Ltd., Ware, Hertfordshire, Great Britain, 1998.

Edited by Kate Rowinski, *The Quotable Mom*, Main Street (division of Sterling Publishing Co. Inc.), New York, 2004.

Compiled by George Seldes, *The Great Quotations*, Lyle Stuart, New York, 1960.

Edited by John M. Shanahan, *The Most Brilliant Thoughts of All Time*, Cliff Street Books (an imprint of HarperCollins Publishers), New York, 1999.

Edited and introduced by Jessie Shiers, *The Quotable Bitch*, The Lyons Press, Guilford, Connecticut, 2008.

Smart Mouths, Portable Press, Ashland, Oregon, 2009.

Edited by Marlo Thomas, *The Right Words at the Right Time*, Atria Books, New York, 2002.

Weekes, Karen, *Women Know Everything!*, Quirk Books, Philadelphia, 2007.

Williams, Ted with David Pietrsza, *My Life in Pictures*, Total/Sports Illustrated, Kingston, New York, 2001.

Compiled and edited by Jon Winokur, *True Confessions*, Dutton, New York, 1992.

Index of Virgos

C

D

K

L

M

N

O

P

R

S

T

U

V

About the Author

Mary Valby's fascination with astrology began as she wrote her Princeton thesis on medieval zodiac signs. Mary has since filtered thousands of books, birthdates, and celebrity comments according to Sun sign. Her astrological pursuits include personalized birth-chart readings, more than a decade maintaining an astrological website, and membership in the American Federation of Astrologers. Raised in upstate New York, Mary now enjoys the Pacific Northwest.

Mary Valby's Astrological Beliefs

- **Real vs. Imaginary.** Astrology works. After cataloguing thousands of celebrities and reading hundreds of charts, Mary fully accepts that astrological placements and movements impact each individual. The celestial sphere proves one of Nature's many guiding cycles.
- **Sun Sign vs. Full Birth-Chart.** The most comprehensive celestial snapshot of your potential comes from a full astrological birth-chart based on time of birth and referencing all solar system planets. The zodiac location of the Sun at your birth indicates far less but remains meaningful. Your Sun sign describes your core energy, the driving life-force that underlies the rest of your personality.
- **Self-Knowledge vs. Prediction.** The better use of astrology is as a tool for self-knowledge. You are not the same as other people; how can you build upon your personal talents while minimizing your weaknesses? Astrology's prediction of favorable and unfavorable periods is most accurate when calculated from a full astrological birth-chart.
- **Free Will vs. Determinism.** Astrology suggests rather than dictates. As if playing a hand of cards, you remain free to choose your responses and actions.

Sun Sign	Usual Dates
Aries	March 21 through April 19
Taurus	April 20 through May 20
Gemini	May 21 through June 20
Cancer	June 21 through July 21
Leo	July 22 through August 22
Virgo	August 23 through September 21
Libra	September 22 through October 22
Scorpio	October 23 through November 22
Sagittarius	November 23 through December 21
Capricorn	December 22 through January 19
Aquarius	January 20 through February 18
Pisces	February 19 through March 20

The dates shown above are the most typical dates for the Sun's yearly passage through each zodiac sign. But the Sun moves into each sign at a specific moment each year, with the dates varying by a day or two from year to year. If you are unsure about the Sun sign for yourself or a person of interest, send date, time and place of birth to help@quotablezodiac.com for a free zodiac identification.

Quick Order Form

Website orders: www.quotablezodiac.com.
Major credit cards accepted.

Email orders: orders@quotablezodiac.com

Postal orders: Quotable Zodiac Publishing, LLC
Mary Valby, P.O. Box 2011, Gig Harbor, WA 98335, USA.
Please send check or money order.

Telephone orders: 253-858-6372, have credit card ready.

The Quotable Zodiac Series

Please send the following books:

____The Quotable Libra ($12.95)
____The Quotable Scorpio ($12.95)
____The Quotable Sagittarius ($12.95)
____The Quotable Capricorn ($12.95)
____The Quotable Aquarius ($12.95)
____The Quotable Pisces ($12.95)
____The Quotable Aries ($12.95)
____The Quotable Taurus ($12.95)
____The Quotable Gemini ($12.95)
____The Quotable Cancer ($12.95)
____The Quotable Leo ($12.95)
____The Quotable Virgo ($12.95)
____Shipping (U.S.): $4.00 for first book and $2.00 for each additional book
____Shipping (International): $9.00 for first book, $5.00 for each additional book
____Total

Name: ______________________________

Address: ______________________________

City: ______________ State: __________ Zip: __________

Telephone: ______________________________

Email address: ______________________________

Send questions or comments to info@quotablezodiac.com